Grace Be

With You

Stirring Truth and Abundant Joy
for Fellow Travelers

Cover art by Rob Connelly. http://heyitsrob.com

Editor's note: Identities and identifying characteristics have been altered in order to maintain anonymity of individuals.

Portions of this book are also from the author's blog and other works.

Scripture quotations are from the Holy Bible, New International Version®, NIV®. Copyright © 1973, 1978, 1984, by International Bible Society. All rights reserved. All quoted Scripture is from the New International Version 1984, and is also God-breathed and useful for teaching, rebuking, correcting, and training in righteousness.

Star Trek quote from "'The Darmok.'" Writ. Joe Menosky, Phillip LaZebnik. *Star Trek: The Next Generation*. CBS. Hollywood, CA: Paramount Studios. September, 28 1991.

Park, J.S., author.
 Grace be with you: stirring truth and abundant joy for fellow travelers / J.S. Park.—First edition.
 Includes bibliographical references.

ISBN 978-0692690314
 1. Christian Poetry, English 2. Inspiration—Religious Aspects—Christianity
 3. Spiritual life—Anecdotes 4. Devotional Literature
 5. Encouragement—Religious Aspects—Christianity—Quotations, Maxims, Etc

Printed in the United States of America.
10 9 8 7 6 5 4 3 2 1

Citation Information:
J.S. Park, *Grace Be With You* (Florida: The Way Everlasting Ministry, 2016) p. _

Join me in the journey of faith.
   Wordpress. jsparkblog.com
   Facebook. facebook.com/pastorjspark
   Tumblr. jspark3000.tumblr.com
   Podcast. thewayeverlasting.libsyn.com
   Twitter. twitter.com/pastorjs3000
   YouTube. youtube.com/user/jsparkblog

Dedicated

To my friend and dear brother,
Andre Holmes,
for being a constant encouragement,
and for always telling me what's real.
You were there through the worst of it,
and you stayed.

Journey of
Contents

Foreword, by T.B. LaBerge

Sometimes we need to hear a story, and the only loving thing we will hear all day is a story from the heart.

I think God is a storyteller; in fact, I know He is. We are living in a story that is so big that we may not know it until eternity, but as we wait for that day, I know that God puts in each of our hearts something to say.

Jesus Christ loved to tell stories to get his message across. I believe that today, stories have become a way of escaping reality, when they were never meant for that. We were told stories because they helped us to see how the world worked, how we are to engage it. They would have lessons of sorrow, love, adventure, and hope. What I love about J.S. Park's stories is that he brings back the lessons. He follows the example of Christ when he tells the simple story of a flat tire, or illustrates our growth by a chisel, or reminds us that no matter how far we have run from Him, it's God's grace that brings us back to Himself. When we are broken down and weary in spirit, it's these little things that bring peace.

You may be in a season of sorrow, in the middle of a storm, you may be lost and confused, but you can always take time to listen to a drop of truth. In an age of self-doubt, we need to hear someone say, "Hang in there, you're going to make it." And in this book, Joon speaks those words we all long to hear.

At the end of all time, I know that every story is woven into the grand story, making its mark as punctuations in the fabric. I hope you may pause to soak in each line, the encouragement that pours out of each page. You may chance upon the lesson that all great stories teach, the reality that you are loved towards a better ending, far beyond what you could have ever hoped for or written.

— **T.B. LaBerge**

Preface:
A Bridge to You and Me, of Purest Stone

There's an old Star Trek episode where a particular alien species, the Tamarians, can only communicate in images and allegories. As the helpful android, Lt. Commander Data, puts it:

> *"Their ability to abstract is highly unusual. They seem to communicate through narrative imagery, a reference to the individuals and places which appear in their mytho-historical accounts."*

This strange constraint plays out to amusing fashion throughout the episode, as each party is frustrated by their miscommunication, and the tension nearly boils over into a knife-fight and all-out war (maybe your idea of amusement is different than mine). By the end, one of the Tamarians sacrifices himself in order to create a heroic narrative that both his people and the Federation can understand. It succeeds; this act of nobility becomes the bridge towards peace. The great Captain Picard realizes, *"The Tamarian was willing to risk all of us, just for the hope of communication—connection."*

We're not much different than the Tamarians. We risk the friction of our jagged edges to connect, not merely by formulas or flowcharts, but by a sloppy crawl through our shared, lived-in journey. We crave a common vocabulary beyond the heavy anvils of prose, crafted from imagination and our unified experiences.

Stories contain power because they seem to unveil secrets that have long been muddled, as if we're unearthing lost royal treasure. But more than that, stories are a connective tissue, bringing us together by the longing and landing of a *resolution*.

Since a narrative thrust is essentially driven by an unresolved tension, with unassailable obstacles besetting a goal on every side, we discover in them the depth of our courage and cowardice, and we find out how *to be*. We find what we're meant to look like.

We find, perhaps unwillingly, that we are not always the heroes, but in need of rescue: because we're so often the cause of our own tension. And this is what puts us in the same boat, the same battle. The best stories require first an examination of our limitations, and then a cooperation as equals, through a slow-burning realization that we are not opposed to one another, but can reach the same goals with a little spunk and ingenuity. From *Star Wars* to *The Karate Kid* to *The Lord of the Rings* to *Up,* from the Epic of Gilgamesh to the *Odyssey* to a genie in a bottle, these are tales told side-by-side. We find we are fellow travelers, not so different, really, with a universal desire for *shalom*, a harmony—and we can't get there alone. Heroes cannot fly solo, and villains are not beyond change.

Stories and symbols have a way of disarming us, too, getting to the inside of the matter with gentle precision. Propositions are a bit like bricks and beams: necessary for the foundation, but soon rigid and inflexible. Narratives and metaphors have a dynamic of growth to them, like seeds pushing through the dirt into the sun, and they give breath. Or maybe, as one theologian said, they are windows that light up the house and give it air. It's why Nathan the prophet did not approach David with lectures and bullet points—"Three reasons that adultery and murder are bad!"—but instead with the innocent story of a poor man and his ewe lamb, ending on a twist that David could not negotiate. It forced David to rise from the dirt, into light.

Jesus himself spoke in parables with great aplomb, from mustard seeds and millstones to swords and sparrows to wedding feasts and rebel-runaways. Jesus's disciples often had trouble deciphering his parables, which Jesus seemed to deliberately obscure at times— but ultimately, the parables were pointing to a future work on a cross and in a tomb. His stories pointed to his heart, and his heart sculpted the greatest story of them all: a final sacrifice to bring us peace with God and one another. He spoke of rescuing us, because we could not do that on our own. We were never meant to.

Only Jesus could become our bridge of peace, our *shalom*. And this kind of love is not merely the royal treasure, but the very purest stone from which all treasures are made.

The following pages are much like rotating the facets of such a jewel, pointing to the pulse of the galaxy-sculptor. These stories and poems and thoughts are chiseled by joy, sorrow, failure—and the great love that has cast a shadow on them all.

Some of the following is from my blog, in which I've compiled the most "viral" writings into four chapters, including new content. The first chapter is to encourage, the second is to stir to action, the third is about the messy middle-space of our journey, and the fourth is to find Christ, our life, everywhere we turn.

My hope is that we meet somewhere between the words, to *connect*, because I believe this is the truest stuff of life. Stories help us to mesh in this tapestry, that in our overlap, we'd find strength hand in hand. I'm excited. I'll see you there.

—J.S.

Hope, Joy, Healing,
and Roller Coasters

Grace is thoughtful. It considers a back-story, an upbringing, the entire person, and not just a tiny single slice of their life.

Grace brings wholeness to a hasty judgment; it regards my own flaws first, in light of the grace I've also been given.

Grace brings what *could be* instead of what should've been. Grace covers my past and empowers my future. It does not condemn nor condone, but convicts and re-creates.

Grace confronts the worst of a person and does not shy away from surgical rebuke, because at our worst, we realize how much we must confront the ugliness inside. But grace restores there, in the wreckage. It is always healing the fractured, fallen, weary sinner. It is not what we deserve, but what we need, and Jesus saw what we deserved, but gave us what we needed instead. That's grace. Love unconditional, undeserved, unrelenting.

Love sees a greatness in someone
who cannot see it in themselves.

You can quit replaying those moments
in your head.
The past is done.
Move forward.
Have grace for yourself.

The fear of moving forward
is often obliterated by moving forward.
Do it scared.

That sudden boost of confidence or euphoria or peace is often because someone just prayed for you. You're on someone's mind. Friends have fasted and written your name down and spoke good intent over you.

It's crazy to think we can tap into the tissue of something greater than ourselves, lending our hearts for strength and healing. Being there is most important, but prayer is for when you can't. It takes a moment. It means a life.

The Whole Story, Ahead and Behind

I saw this very slow car on the interstate in front of me that was rusted through and ready to fall apart, and for some reason, I was overly irritated at someone driving so slow in such a beat-up car. It must have been going 40 in a 65 mph zone.

I passed and pulled up next to the car, and I got a glance of the lady inside. Suddenly I felt terrible. Her face looked absolutely wrecked and tragic, like she had just heard the worst news in the world. Her shoulders were fallen into a heap and her mouth was open and her eyes were glass and mist, not quite weeping but just holding back. She was staring into nothing. I've been there. I know what that's like, the hurt pulling in through your lungs and the bottom dropped out. It turns the world into gray noise. Completely numb and unable to see how it could possibly get better.

I got behind the lady again to follow her and make sure she was okay. She got off the interstate safely. I thought that maybe if other drivers were going to get mad at her, they could get mad at me first. It all changes when you know what a person is going through.

A Bad Day / A Good Day

My car got another flat again, my fourth one in a year, and I needed to get towed. My spare was also flat and I was on the side of the interstate with giant trucks flying by. I was pretty bummed out about the whole thing, because financially I was in a rough place and was dog-sick with a cold, the kind with green snot and evil-witch-coughing.

The lady on the phone from roadside service gave me the reference number 5377, and said, "You're the five-thousand three-hundred seventy-seventh caller today, so you're not the only one having a bad day." We both laughed. I totally unclenched after that—and it wasn't that I wanted other people to have a bad day, but I imagined all these strangers on the side of the road with their broke-down cars, shaking their heads with me in unison, and the image brought a weird comfort, like dipping my toes in the water during a heat wave. I put my phone away and watched the clouds for a while. I realized I hadn't looked up at the sky for a long time.

The tow truck driver was with his mom, who was living at a shelter for abused women. The driver took his mom to work on every tow, to keep her company. We talked about my wedding and about being a pastor. Then the driver told some jokes and his mom and I couldn't stop laughing; I was honestly embarrassed to laugh so hard. I already knew some of the jokes but I didn't stop him. We got to the car shop and I gave him all the cash I had for tip, ten bucks, and he thanked me like crazy. The mom shouted out, "Best of luck with your marriage!"— and I waved as big as I could.

I guess bad days can get turned around with good people. Those days, I have to look up to notice.

You're Doing a Good Thing

Most testimonies of victory have a turning point, which usually sounds like, "And then I met this pastor," or "Then this counselor came by," or "I got this text at the perfect time." It seems random, but those encounters and calls and messages of encouragement happened on purpose. Someone made a choice to reach out, get involved, get near another person's wreckage, and help them for one more step. It was enough to get them moving again.

I was having this really hard week, and I found a note in my backpack. No name or anything, just, *"You're doing a good thing. I'm with you."* And as silly as it sounds, I got emotional. Someone took their time to notice my mood, grab a pen and some paper, write out this thoughtful little note, and secretly stuff it in my backpack. It changed my week. I stood a bit taller. You never know what these kinds of things can do for someone. And it only takes a few seconds to breathe that sort of life into a tired soul.

Maybe it was no big deal for the person who reached out. But to the person they helped, it meant everything. It was the turning point. It was the beginning of seeing new light, of finding a new dream, the start of healing. A little bit of your time and wisdom might turn someone's life around. You never know: so go.

A Galaxy in a Cup, a Memory of the Future

I have a past that I'm not very proud of, and in a cafe, I saw someone from my past for just a flash of a second.

It was all I needed to remember. In that tiny compact parcel of a second, I replayed every terrible, awful, humiliating moment of self-indulgent excess in a nause-ating loop, both the ways I used people and was used, and then: shame. Drowning shame. That awful sick-stomach feeling of tendrils racing up my gut, a stench that begins at the back of the throat to the tip of my nostrils, like choking in reverse.

A Christian might call this "condemnation." I also call it "standing naked in town hall with every hurtful thing you've ever done on the wall, and also it's very cold in there."

Slipping, I reached for something in my head, finger-nails scratching through a narrowing stone tunnel, spinning, up now down, the verdict pressing in, chains tightening. I felt like that guy on the news who has microphones shoved in his face after a scandal; you know, the carnival games were rigged the whole time, how dare you, you monster. Voices crowded in, the chorus shouting, "You're not any different, you haven't changed, I know who you really are"—and somewhere in that mess of lies, I found it.

It's sort of trite maybe, and one of those moments I groan at during an inspirational Sunday service. But I thought of the verse: *"Therefore, if anyone is in Christ, he is a new creation; the old has gone, the new has come."*

I remember researching this once, and Paul was so excited when he wrote this verse that he skipped all the verbs. Which was very unlike the eloquent Paul. So it actually says, "Therefore anyone Christ, he new creation; old gone, new here."

I'm imagining how liberating and heart-rending this was for Paul, who once killed Christians for a living and was probably serving at churches where there were family members of people he had persecuted. I'm imagining his nightmares and the regret over people he hurt. I'm envisioning his tears and apologies and humility for these families, only for them to say, "You've been re-made, Paul. You're not who you were. You're new." I'm thinking of how much this tenderized him and galvanized him.

That's what Christians call "grace." It's the hope of an undeserved love so that we can bear to be vulnerable in honesty and intimacy. It's what we crave most and what we're least willing to give. Yet God, we're told, is willing to give it freely, at a cost to Himself, wave after wave of that stuff, like galaxies in a cup.

It doesn't mean we're not accountable or that everything is just fine. Of course, there must be reparations and reconciliation. But it does mean we're no longer imprisoned to compensating for the shame of the "old-me." I'm not bound to paying off my record by faking some kind of head-hanging modesty. The old-me is dead. The old-you is gone. It takes no less than the piercing love of God to put it to death, to die. It takes no less than the restoring love of God to give us breath, to make us alive. That's the only thing I know that keeps me humble and fills me with confidence at the same time. It's how we stop tumbling, and stand.

In Christ, no one is ever the same person they were before. It means that I don't forget where I came from, but I can't forget where I'm going.

The shame lifted then. Not all the way. Maybe enough to breathe a little. Maybe enough to fight back the voices. Maybe enough to still the past, and reach for hope, for a memory of the future. And that was enough.

Lord, this prayer is for anyone —
with a pair of bruised hands and baggage-burned eyes,
a thousand pound soul and languished sighs.
If you're bound up, shackled up, beat down, held down,
giving in, giving up, at the limit, at the end
—just stay a step. One more.
God, receive us, free us, renew our senses, put the color
back into things, to taste the dimmest light seeping in.
Give back to us something like joy and motion.
Not "how it used to be,"
but the flip of a page, the next chapter,
the ready texture of a blank white sheet ready for the
feather-dipped black to begin again.
Lord, this prayer is for anyone.

Oceans, Motion, Joy

To see a marriage so bubbling and intimate and alive, to see a business with its interlocking efficiency, to see a work of art filled with splashing colors and the smallest of lines—none of these things happened out of whimsy.

We can look at a picture of life in motion and assume that it was instant magic. We're tickled by "love at first sight" because it stirs our easy-button of convenience. And it looks like luck falls out of the sky for everyone else.

But—dreams take sweat and scars and apologies. Hopes are stitched with false starts and valleys of failure. The ease of intimacy you see in a single conversation took many, many turns through the desert. Romance is not romantic. A building begins with the smashing of elbows and hammers. Our art, whether song or dance or writing or film or poetry, takes months of anxious labor. The band you see on stage rocking the stadium spent directionless weekends in pubs in front of disinterested strangers. Art is never born from safety and stillness.

Please don't be fooled by the seduction of bite-sized daydreams. Real dreams begin with dirt, with intensity. Don't be taken in by the highlights of social media. They may fuel you, but life needs you to be all there. And when you've pushed past the initial illusion of lake-shallow emotions, you will find an ocean of richness and depth that was worth the pain, worth the risk, worth your tears and busted seams. There, you will find the deepest laughter. There is a joy that hurts.

We're tempted by a future where we've finally arrived to the big time—but maybe this is it, this moment, where we're called to be completely engaged and totally present, eye to eye, face to face, heart to heart, with the few. To change even one life *is* the big time.

Our efforts and networking and connections don't always have to pay off. We plant seeds everywhere that we're fully there. The fruits will come. Sometimes the fruit is you.

If you're not sure how to make a certain decision, consider how you'll look back on what you decided. Look back on it from your future self.

If you want to take that memory with you, then brave every risk and climb every cliff—do what it takes to get there. Give your future the best hope of nostalgia.

If you know your decision will be a burden of baggage, then hold on to what you must and let go of what controls you. You have just the one story to tell, but most importantly, it's the only story you must one day tell yourself. Make it the one you want.

I'm learning that faithfulness is more important than fruitfulness, because even when there are no results and rewards, I'm still meant to run this race.

Yet I'm also learning that most of the race will be hard work, in silence, amidst people who often don't care, with little evidence that we're making a difference and many failed heartbreaks of seeing others walk away.

I'm learning this can be a cruel, thoughtless, heartless world, and to be a fleeting flash of light is so much better, and so rare. I'm learning again and again to trust God for what I cannot see, because He's the only one who heals hearts to glory. I'm learning to encourage others along the way, because so many never get to hear that they're doing all right, and I want to be the one voice in the crowd that actually breathes life, even when it's for a second and forgotten.

Trust that God is working something in you now,
something you can't imagine,
a miracle beyond proportion.
Look beyond circumstances, long nights,
broken trophies, mental arguments, the swirl of gossip,
the false self-talk that you've rehearsed over and over.
Leave yesterday where it belongs.
Don't cave in to what has happened to you.
God says you are more than that —
because you are His.
As hard as it sounds:
you are loved, you are treasured,
you are written on the heart and mind of your Creator.
Rejoice and revel in what He has done,
is doing,
will do.

Take as long as it takes. Please don't be rushed into a decision, an emotion, an opinion, the very next thing. No one else has to live what you decide. They will move on long after you've pleased them; you must sculpt with your own chisel.

One time after church, I texted this girl, "You looked great today," and she didn't reply. And then I felt horribly stupid, like just beat-myself-up stupid. You know, that swimmy sick-to-your-stomach anxiety when you want to jump out the window with a desk tied to your leg. I mean who even says that out loud to another person? I kept repeating it in my head over and over in the most nasal voice possible—You looked great today!—and doing the corny Yeah-You-Betcha wink. I lost sleep. I had that late-night regret twitch where I wanted to punch myself to never do it again. The cool thing is that now we're married.

I was a college drop-out with a 0.9 GPA who lost a scholarship and took seven years to graduate after going to two community colleges. It doesn't matter how long it takes, everyone blooms differently. Setbacks are not failures and you are more than yesterday. Own your mistakes, quit the inner-loop of shaming in your head, smile big, move on.

If you must look to the past:
look to learn and to laugh.

If you must look to the future:
look to go forward, not back.

And if you must look to this moment:
consider right now is all you will have.

The Clouds Part and We Ride the Summit

There are days or weeks or even months when I read the Bible and there are no grand epiphanies.

There are whole seasons of Sundays when I sing praise and feel nothing.

There are times of prayer where the silence kills me. There are great Christian books and podcasts that I eat up which don't budge my spiritual life.

There are too many times when I doubt the very existence of God and the sending of His Son. It can all feel like a crazy lie.

It's in those times that I ask myself, "Am I out of love with God somehow? Am I losing my faith here? How do I get back to where I used to be?"

But I keep reading my Bible. I keep singing on Sundays. I keep praying. I soak in books and sermons. I serve. I enjoy the company of mature Christians. I enjoy the fellowship of the broken.

And you know, sometimes the clouds part and God comes through and His love squeezes my heart and I fall to my knees remembering how good He is. Then I read Scripture and can't stop weeping and I turn on Christian songs in my car full blast and sing loud enough to scare the traffic. I serve with shaking hands and get convicted by those sermons and soak in God's goodness all over again.

So I've learned over time: *I wasn't really out of love with God. I'm just a fragile human being who changes as much as the weather. I was setting a ridiculous standard for myself that can't be defined by self-pressuring parameters. I was tricked by the enemy into judging my flesh. How I feel is important, but it's not the whole basis of my faith. It's wholly, solely, defiantly by His grace—and in that, I think I can finally relax.*

When you return to God after a long time away, He doesn't judge or keep score. In fact, it's His very acceptance that will restore you back to intimacy again. His very grace heals you back to Himself.

Jaded and Worn Down, Waiting on God Again

The other night, I was at a church service and I was really asking God to do something.

I was getting jaded. Really, really worn down. I had that sour cynicism: *I've already heard every kind of sermon there is, I know all the right theology, I've read every bestseller, I know all the songs and what they'll say next.* It's a bad place to be. It feels like I've tapped out on faith and I would never get back to that fiery, from-the-gut connection that I used to have. I've gotten out of it before, but maybe this time, I would have to learn how to settle. I guess it would be okay.

This song came on. I've heard it before. I've heard it a billion times. But the second I sang the lyrics, "the Glory of God," I totally lost it. I mean really, like I was blubbering in a dark room with hundreds of other people hoping they wouldn't look. They looked. I didn't care. I sang glory until my throat rolled over. I could see dust spinning in the projector; I don't know why but it made me weep harder.

I know that emotions and all that don't mean everything. It's just that I was really thinking of glory, of the overpowering, overwhelming, unbearable weight of God. The galaxy-sculptor. The infuser of oxygen and orbits and musical chords. I got this really big picture of God for a moment. I was dust in a sunbeam. And I thought of Him touching the dirt of the earth, breathing the same air and singing the same songs, a God so big and yet so close, a glorious God who threw stars into space and bled in my place—and for a while, it was hard to handle. A huge God, yet intimately here.

I knew I hadn't even begun to approach the surface of an infinitely vast God. I'm glad for that. I'm glad that my tiny, squishy, fragile, little brain could even comprehend a tenth of a tenth of a tenth of Him. He's that good. He's enough for an endless heart that's wired for eternity.

Farewell, Honeymoon Valley

Many of us put absurd, arbitrary goal-lines on our "spiritual walk" so we expect to sustain how we first felt. But a true, long-term, sustainable faith will never feel like it first did. How could it? Coming to faith in Christ is always exciting—but keeping up that level of emotionalism is impossible. The Sunday-pep-rally fervor can't top itself every week.

Think of a hit TV show in its first season. New characters, scenarios, dialogue: it's all so fresh and thrilling. But even when it maintains high quality, it'll be a little stale by the third season, because we become so familiar with the tropes and twists and writing.

Think of a marriage: the honeymoon phase. Some of us expect the "butterflies" and "electricity" to keep going. When it doesn't, it leads to disillusionment or worse. If you tried to have a wedding every day of your marriage, it would get exhausting.

Moses didn't split the Red Sea every Thursday. David didn't conquer Goliath at every revival. And Jesus didn't transfigure at every luncheon.

The Bible never calls us to continually duplicate our highs. We're called to remember the Most High in our lows. We can only be reminded that **Jesus is present in both our mountaintops and valleys.** *Some days are Romans 7, some Romans 8, and He is in both.*

The Christian life is your *whole life*. That sin which keeps defeating you has more roots than you think, and God is patient to work in you for the surgery.

Our journey of faith is a growing process of fits and starts, aches and pains, highs and lows, bliss and blisters. Jesus is going to take you all the way home on this. Keep leaning in with the full weight of your weary, desperate soul. He will catch you, always.

The Moment After Defeat

Maybe you totally blew it today. That Sunday sermon about peace and patience and purity totally convicted you, and you promised to God for the fiftieth time that you'd re-double your grit and fortitude. But you messed it up. You lost it in traffic, went off on your family, went on that website, used again. You thought, "I'm a fake, a phony, a fraud. Who am I fooling? I know how I really am, and that can't change"—except, that's life. You were always going to fail. You were going to need a hand up. It's the very reason Jesus had to die for you, and was glad to.

So you had a good run and fell flat on your face: but by faith we are no longer under condemnation, we are being re-created in the image of our God, His mercies are new every morning, and He who began a good work in you will carry it unto completion. The outer flesh is perishing but the inner-you is being renewed day by day, and you are not where you could be, but you are not where you once were.

Through all of it, God won't change on you, and that's how you will. Press into Him on that, and He is gracious for another opportunity to give over the glory, however imperfectly. Get up, go again. Make it right where you can; learn from where you can't, and trust Him for tomorrow. The moment of defeat matters less than the moment after. That's when you need Him most, and that's when He does his best. The story ain't over.

Grace to Rest, to Fight

True grace is both our **haven of rest** and **resolve to fight**.

It's rest. It's to know that our desperation for validation is already found in all that God has done for us. It's work *from* God's approval and not *for*. We can quit playing games of achievement and side-eye comparison and one-upmanship. We can quit living for ourselves under the weight of an egotistical tyranny. We can quit trying to pay off the gap between *who-we-are* and *who-we-want-to-be*.

Yet—it's resolve. Grace motivates us into the true versions of ourselves, by the motivation of no-motivation, because we are not trying to "get better" for the sake of improvement, but becoming better by clinging to the Only One who is good. It's to leave behind the corpse of the old-me, for that wretchedness died with Jesus's love for me. We are motivated by beauty rather than practicality, because the love of God is entirely intrinsic unto itself, in a single direction initiated by its own essence, with nothing to gain and no reason to exist except that it does. It disturbs our ego and complacency; it is the limitless love that provokes us into the same love.

This way takes longer, but its roots grow deeper. It is harder to preach, but its proclamation is what truly transforms.

The heart of God
will never change
no matter what you do,
and it's His unchanging heart
that changes you.

Don't settle for less.
Don't sell yourself short.
Don't be rushed into a feeling,
a decision, an opinion.
Don't let anyone talk you down.
Drop the mic often.
Prioritize, for our time on earth is short.
Think for yourself.
Find your vision. Listen.
Do not hide tears; they're yours.
Trust God. Take heart. Keep passion.
Fight the good fight, fellow traveler.
Fight.

The Perpetual Time-Stamp Loop

I often imagine what other people in my small, tiny town are saying about me, in a hushed backroom of seedy rumors. It's a bit self-indulgent, but no less debilitating.

You're not the good guy you pretend to be.

I know who you really are.

I know what you're about.

You're not fooling anyone.

I get into a mental chokehold, a constant tortured paralysis, not allowing myself any joy for too long, because I feel that's a righteous punishment.

Are we all doomed to our former selves, time-stamped to who we used to be? Will this loop of self-condemnation never end?

Having been in the same town for a long time, I've learned no one likes to flip the page, because cynicism appeals to our laziness. It's less work to bury someone under their baggage than to help them unpack. We write someone off and dismiss them because it's easy, natural, cut from the complacency of flesh.

But if we were to sit down for an hour over coffee, maybe we'd understand a bit more. That we have the same hopes, dreams, passions, and ambitions. That we are surprisingly similar. That we've both failed. We both have a past. That we love children, love dogs, love good movies, enjoy coffee, laugh at viral videos, and weep at tragic headlines. That we share fears, addictions, complexes, and worries. You'd certainly see horrible things in me, but perhaps you'd feel love instead of judgment, the same love you'd want for yourself.

And we'd see we are both multi-dimensional people who fight the same battles with our multiple, split selves, and that we're not stock archetypes from a backyard Disney vault. We are gritty and imperfect: just people.

Maybe we'd get to know each other's honest conflict inside, and recognize that we both don't always get it right, and we could meet there, in our failures and the next step forward.

Of course, you and I may never get to share our side of the story. No one might believe you've changed. Even when you do the right thing, others might assume you're doing it to get ahead or to show off. When you do wrong, it might confirm a pre-engraved bias that was set in stone before you got there. Maybe no one will see you're striving for sincerity, that you've become more patient and humble and gracious than you've ever been.

That's okay. We can still have grace for the people who don't. You can do your best when others won't. And it's His testimony, anyway. His work through you is what will shine through, and His glory will speak louder than dishonor: for even a ridiculed hometown prophet was honored, in the end.

I know that problem feels unbeatable right now. Where you want to be feels far away. Your numbness is growing, your heart hardens, the chasm deepens. You wonder why you keep trying, when it'll pay off, when your steps forward will be more than the steps back.

Please don't give up.

When it seems most difficult, the breakthrough is over the next hill. The freedom from your old self is very, very near, and once you taste it, the effort will have been more than worth it.

Those who gave up were always just two breaths away.

Progress gets harder because you're getting better.

Only look behind you to see how far you've traveled, to see the lessons learned and the laughter had. Otherwise: eyes ahead.

Don't give in now. You're further along than you think. And even in your stumbling, you are tasting the freedom of moving forward.

Hang in there.

This world is not our final home.

Do something; move on.

Meanwhile: Start

You might have had a picture of how you wanted your life to be, but some uncontrollable tragedy swept it away. We all have a certain picture of how we want our lives to be, and sometimes it gets ripped from our grip and smashed to pieces. Our dreams can get crushed in an instant, in the most horrible ways, with irreversible results.

We might be living in a life right now that doesn't feel like it's ours, you and I. We might be in a different place than we had hoped for. Today could be different than you had imagined and planned a year ago. Your heart will pull for another chance, another door, another world. We wake up in a daze, wondering how things changed so fast. We wait, hoping it'll go back to the way it was. The three hardest words to live with are often: In the meantime.

Yet—in the meantime is the whole thing. If you're waiting for your "real life" to start, after graduation or when you're married or when you get to the big city, you'll stay in a holding pattern. The time will pass anyway. The tide doesn't wait.

So I hope you'll consider starting in the meanwhile. When a dream dies, it dies. We can mourn. We can pound our chest. We can bleed. And at some point, we must let go and not linger. You can open your hands to another dream. I hope you find this new dream. I hope you don't try to revive something that's dead.

You can get over what's over, because you're not over yet. When the ten count is over, you can count to eleven. What comes next will not be what you had envisioned. It might be better or it might be worse. I hope you will keep dreaming anyway. I hope you will consider God can do a new thing.

You are free to pursue something new.

Forgetting How to Be,
Reclaiming How to Breathe

I met with my counselor the other day, a semi-famous mega-church pastor here in town, and I had really forgotten what it's like to be around someone who is so comfortable with himself that it made me comfortable with myself.

My counselor is one of those cool pastors who smokes cigars and uses dirty words and he used to be a rich drug dealer, so he owns this huge house and hosts these extravagant church parties with hundreds of curious people looking for real spirituality. He does this without even really trying to impress anyone, and with sort of a wink. Once I was leaving his office after a meet and he yells down the hallway of his church, "I'll keep praying about your porn problem." The very conservative staff glanced at me and I ran and he couldn't stop laughing. My counselor reminds me of Jesus.

So I told him everything. How I blew up on someone the other day. How I was juggling multiple ministries plus a growing blog. How dissatisfied I was with the mainstream church. How I haven't talked to my dad in over a year. How I was fighting anger and unforgiveness and lust. How I always felt like I was pouring out of an empty cup, and that the same grace I preached for others was almost never reserved for myself.

I told him I had this monster inside me, barely underneath the surface just coiled around my guts, and just when I thought I was making "Christian progress" and it was dead, it would lash out and destroy everything I love and then go right back to hiding. I wanted this thing inside me to really, truly, eternally die.

Then he looks at me and says, "You're not really walking with God."

I was almost offended. But he was right. He went on.

"You're doing so much, just do, and you lost who you are. You find who you are, then you can do again."

"So what do I do now?" As soon as I said it, I heard it. I said "do" again.

He said, "Pray. I mean we're both in ministry, you already know that. But you see how we're talking? How you can tell me anything? How I can just be me around you? That's prayer. Praying is like breathing. It's a way of life that can happen all the time. That's walking with Him."

I think I was trying not to weep. I remember when it was like that, when I felt like I was walking with Him all the time. When being with God was like breathing. I did want that again. And it was not a matter of doing, but being.

He said, "It's okay to pour out when you're empty. You can't do that for a long time, but that's grace. You can preach grace all day and be a legalist to yourself. Quit listening to yourself and listen to Him. And don't preach too far ahead of yourself. If it's been hard, then preach that it's been hard."

We hugged for a long time. He told me he loved me. Before we parted, he said, "I wish I could tear that monster out of you. Let God inside, and He will."

The Christian is a work in progress,
looking towards the work finished,
Jesus.

Please do not inject a false narrative into your life based on your mood, one day, or one week, thinking the whole thing is who you are and how life is always going to be. Sometimes I feel like this is always how it's going to feel like—and that isn't true.

You're allowed to have a bad day. Even a bad week, a bad month, a bad long season.

Just don't let it say everything about you. A bad day is not you.

Waves, Night, The End

I was walking along the beach tonight, wave after wave rushing at the side of my toes.

I saw a light at the end of the shore, a tiny dot, and I thought about the end.

I saw people swimming, clapping, dancing, kissing, fighting on the sand. I thought about taking a part in those lives, the swirling stories and journeys and conflict all colliding; I thought about the crying and joy and laughter and paint-brushed moments like they were made just for us; I thought of births and weddings and funerals, places where people hug.

I saw the invisible clock on our foreheads counting back to zero and the sound of the book closing shut on the last page of our lives.

I thought about the people who lied to me, hurt me, betrayed me, stole me—and I was mad, but I was sad too, because they need another chance as much as I do.

I thought of being old, wrinkles on my eyelids, and how much I'd love my wife as her hair goes gray, and if my kids would say that I did okay as my frail fingers held their fresh hands, and if my last whisper would be something funny or something wise.

I thought of God, watching us grow up, a proud Father who felt our stumbles and picked us up again, even when we refused, and His very breath lighting up my lungs like the way the moon hit the end of each wave as it broke along the shore.

I saw the light at the end of the beach again, and thought about the other side of those lights, to a strange eternal place called home, where I could keep my toes in the sand forever.

I looked at the waves, wave after wave, endless in their relentless supply, and I thought of grace.

I walked back to my car. My life was a little past halfway done.

I want to end it right.

I want to fight this fight.

I need the waves this night.

I need grace.

Today you were defeated,
discouraged, dejected, burned again.
Someone brought it up, dressed you down
told you off, staged a coup.
Any other day you could've shrugged it off:
but not today.
A tone, a word, a face dragged you into a pit,
a chokehold, a fog.
It stings. But hey: you are not what has happened to you.
You're not someone else's fake idea
of who they think you should be.
You're more than a backroom whisper
where rumors lose reality
—you are more than seedy surface opinions
born in a broth of fantasy.
You are beloved by a cosmic king of constancy
who has narrated a different history over today,
and every day, and for eternity.
He underlines, highlights, italicizes you
apart from who you think you are:
and He is writing you with a furious final love.
Don't let a bad mood steal you;
don't let a bad day say more about you than today.
Because it's just today.
Let love say good morning.

"Not that I have already obtained all this,
or have already been made perfect,
but I press on to take hold
of that for which Christ Jesus took hold of me.
Brothers, I do not consider myself yet
to have taken hold of it.
But one thing I do:
Forgetting what is behind
and straining toward what is ahead,
I press on toward the goal to win the prize
for which God has called me heavenward
in Christ Jesus."
— Philippians 3:12-14

"For it is by grace you have been saved,
through faith —
and this not from yourselves,
it is the gift of God —
not by works, so that no one can boast.
For we are God's workmanship,
created in Christ Jesus to do good works,
which God prepared in advance
for us to do."
— Ephesians 2:8-10

Truth, Conviction,
and Midnight Epiphanies

Love does not pamper.

It prunes and perfects and pursues.

It is a sweet embrace and a sanctifying chisel.

Note to future self:
When you don't get it right—
Apologize quickly and let go.
Don't beat yourself up
or defend yourself too long.
Humans are squishy with small brains.
We don't get it right every time.
And that's okay.
Being wrong is not the end of the world.

Whenever I think in a sermon, "I wish my friend would get this"—I have to remember it's for me first. Not for the guy five rows down. Not for my parents, not for the pastor, not for "my generation." It starts with me, with you, with owning our part.

Hope for Those Punk Kids At Church (Like Me)

I visited a mega-church and I sat behind a group of college and high school students who were goofing off and checking their phones and leaving early. One of their mothers left in the middle of the sermon and didn't come back. I started getting terribly sad and angry about the whole thing; they all had Bibles in their hands and some had notepads to take notes, but they were just being rowdy and whispering loudly and laughing at the most inappropriate times. I thought, *This is it, this is our future of the church. No one cares.*

And then—I remembered when I was in high school and college, and how much I goofed off and talked during the sermon and was so dang fidgety and rowdy, and how God still worked through a young, rebellious punk like me. I remembered how God had side-tackled me into pastoral ministry and pulverized my heart into a Jesus-loving, people-serving, unabashed follower. Not perfect, never, but far from where I used to be in the very same place as those kids.

So I stopped judging and I started praying. I prayed for big visions for all of them, that God would do incredible, wonderful things that they could barely believe were happening—amazing works that they never thought possible. I mean, if I went back to my past self ten years ago and said, "Here's what you're going to do for God," I never would've believed it. But this is what Jesus does. He takes the most ragged, rowdy, unlikely wanderer and puts us on the frontlines to flex His glory, to wield His love, to heal people just like us. He's always doing things like that, His heart so patient and pursuing.

I get so weary trying to love people. It takes everything. Humility can feel like humiliation. Patience feels like losing. Grace can feel like pain.

But the alternative is far worse. It's hard to love people, but so much harder not to. Hate feels like winning but it shuts the door. Grace is the only seed that might bloom. Either way there's a cost, so I choose to invest in love.

If churches were run like hospitals, we might see the urgency of emergency and lay down our petty bickering. Jesus is for the wounded; we must be, too.

Beggars and Choosers

At the homeless ministry, when volunteers say "Beggars can't be choosers," I always say:

"No, they totally can."

I don't mean that being spoiled is okay, but the homeless have preferences and likes and dislikes, like everyone else. Sometimes they don't want the pasta or the mashed potatoes or the tuna casserole and they just want the salad. They don't always want your really old, used-up walkman or your backpack from middle school. And not every homeless person is there to ego-boost some wealthy person's savior-narrative. They want the same respect and humanity and dignity we all do.

Starbucks Preacher

I saw a pastor with his Bible open at Starbucks teaching theology to another guy, who was a random stranger he happened to meet that day. The pastor was unloading all kinds of information about creation and moral laws and prophecies and pneumatology and atonement, and it was all very good and knowledgeable and I applaud him for that—but I guess the one thing I would've done differently is just to ask questions.

"What's always bothered you about Christianity? How's your church experience been? How's everything going with you? Do you want me to pray for anything?"

I don't mean to diminish this pastor, and it's actually really hard to do what he was doing. I just wonder how many times I tried teaching someone all my impressive information without listening first. I wonder how long I let myself get into lecture-mode without really caring about my fellow human being who didn't need extra theology, but needed the theology to be me, by his side.

The only time a Christian should be first is when they're the first to apologize, first to confess their mistakes, first to care and humble themselves.

Never to compare or compete with another's worth, because we got the heavenly riches and it's enough to go around: first.

The Longest Plank Is Your Own

Unless someone is willing to see the unwieldy plank in their own eye, it's absolutely impossible to help them out of their destructive patterns and self-deception.

You can yell and grieve and make a scene. You can spend hours in gentle counsel and eloquent exchange and loud weeping and tongue-biting patience. But unless that person wants to change, it's not happening. No argument or mercy or fervency is enough. They'll need to be pierced by their own convictions, or in the worst case, they must come to their own ruin and see the miles of hurt they've caused. Otherwise, you're only reinforcing their pride and building their defenses and rationalizations.

Often the only thing we can do is to pray and humble ourselves. To look at our own plank first. To expect the best, even if the other person is taking no strides. To keep the door open. To keep serving. And maybe it's not about the other person, anyway. If they don't change, you will.

If You Knew How It Really Is

Back in my college years, when I was still the worst kind of kid, I was with my friend at this pizza place. This guy and a woman was in another booth across the restaurant, and we were the only ones there. The guy kept staring at me with a hard look.

I got a little angry. You know, that young sort of anger when you think someone is trying to size you up. Maybe he thought I was looking at his girlfriend, or I had bumped into him in the line. I kept staring back.

Then I yelled out, "Why do you keep looking at me, man? You got a problem over here?"

The guy looked away, and I thought: *I win, punk.* The woman stood up and walked over to my table. *Oh, great. His girlfriend is going to defend his honor.*

But the woman was much older, and she leaned in and said, "That's my son. He has Down syndrome. He just thought you were interesting because of your hair."

I had an urge to jump under the table and die.

"I'm really sorry," I said. "I'm sorry."

The woman walked back. I looked at her son and he was staring at his pizza, with the same look he had given me.

My friend took a bite of his pizza and said, "You never know, huh? There's always a twist."

Some days I pray, "Lord, have mercy on me, a sinner." Other days it's, "Lord, please slap me upside the head, for I am an idiot."

Dialogue, Maybe Over Coffee

A blogger once completely destroyed my entire blog. He wrote a detailed analysis of the whole thing, from my theology to posts to quotes to my childhood.

He actually had great points, and I imagine that if we sat down for coffee and discussed these things, we would find a lot of common ground. I had to really think about some areas that I mishandled. My only issue, really, was that he was so very distasteful and trashy and condescending that I just couldn't take him very seriously. I'm afraid I've fallen into the same trap of just going off on someone online, especially when I've had a bad day—and I can't blame it on that so much, either. A lot of the times, it's just me.

Even when someone offers fair criticism, I'm not always sure they're interested in actual dialogue. There's about a zero percent chance it will be a healthy talk, anyway. The more you defend and explain, the more it's misinterpreted. If you miss a single thing, it will be pounced on and torn to pieces. If you apologize, it's never enough. Semantics always escalate. And I learned: Christians love to devour their own. There's some epidemic of Christian men who love to watch other Christian men burn (cue the Hans Zimmer horns).

Tone, approach, and demeanor are all crucial to being heard. I can't hear someone who makes a million assumptions with the subtlety of a sledgehammer. It doesn't matter that we agree or disagree. My question is: *Would you listen to you if you spoke the same way to yourself?*

I've failed at this many times, and I want to do better.

I love conversation. I love to be challenged. I think even conflict with a direction can lead to growth. The point isn't to see eye to eye. The point is to lay down our presumptions and to grow from the best of each other. It's to not make a false parody of the other viewpoint, but to truly listen, and then to offer an angle that hasn't been considered. It's to humanize someone so that we're not equating disagreement with moral value. It's to first consider that we don't see the whole thing ourselves, and maybe the meeting of our perspectives can create an even higher ground to see more than before.

Of course, it has to start with a sensible approach on both sides, and the willingness to be teachable. If your mind is already made up, then never mind. We don't have to like each other, but there's a huge difference between winning points for preaching to the choir and actually caring about the truth. There's a difference between proving the point right and proving yourself right. One gets heard; the other gets a shrug. We don't have to agree. I just want to talk, over coffee.

You'll either be a voice
that someone has to overcome —
Or you'll be a voice
that helps someone overcome.
Each moment, you choose.

Jesus Keeping It Real Keeps Us Real

Jesus said some really hard things that we tend to skip over.

He said it's better to cut off your hand to stop sinning than to enter hell with two healthy hands. Is that a metaphor? Or Jesus keeping it real?

He talked about a place of unceasing anguish and tormenting fire, where "the worm never dies." In the original Greek language, by worms—he meant worms. The kind that eats dead things. Is that a metaphor? Or Jesus keeping it real?

He said anyone who causes someone to stumble should tie a millstone around their necks and throw themselves in the ocean. Millstones weighed up to half a ton. Jesus probably said this while pointing to an actual millstone, because all good preachers use object illustrations. Can we really allegorize that one?

I think we easily dress up Jesus as a doe-eyed, haloed, well-manicured surfer holding dry-cleaned sheep who said things like "I love you no matter what" all the time—and while it's absolutely true that he loves us no matter what, *the love of Jesus was absolutely ferocious, life-changing, and heart-rending.* Anyone who met Jesus would never, ever be the same. There's no neutral reaction to him, or else we haven't met him.

And if a place like Hell really existed, how could Jesus talk about anything else? How was he not going crazy just grabbing people and screaming in their face about it? If love is the most important reality of humanity and Jesus truly embodied love, how was he not talking about millstones all the time?

In Jesus, I read these hard things as if he had tears in his eyes, weeping over his people—and, in fact, he did (Luke 19:41, John 11:35). Jesus was a man of mercy, but also a man of sorrows: because so often both must be coupled together. If he was desperate to tell us the truth of the universe, then his extreme examples make sense. There was probably no human language that could exaggerate such love and grief.

Jesus knew our temptation would be to sugarcoat him, to lower the bar on his holiness until such disproportion would blind us from his piercing, surgical love. He knew I would wiggle my way out by countering, "Well I like this thing you said, but not that one," until we mold God in our own image. I turn Him into a tiny two-inch keychain, and I would reject that god, too. It's a phantom I can dismiss at my convenience. Imagine that every time my wife disagreed with me, I pressed a mute-button and she could no longer stop me. Then I wouldn't have a wife; she would be an accessory.

This is why the God of the Bible is His very own real being, because at some point, He will inevitably press in on a chronologically confined tradition of culture and shake up the familiar areas that we've taken for granted. I would expect nothing less. **This is not a God you can make up as you go along.** *He has a mind that will run full speed through yours.* He will tear down old walls and build entirely new worlds in you, and it will be both agonizing and liberating.

You only need to imagine a time traveler from a thousand years in the future, who will find some of our methods unthinkably barbaric: and even more so, God is timeless, from all times, and His way is perfect, and He holds eternity while we each have one chance on earth to really know Him. It's no wonder he was so desperate, gracious, bold, and urgent, all at once.

If we really do have a God with His own thoughts and dreams and hopes, and if He is after our very best no matter what the cost, **we need to allow God to challenge and offend and press in on our most preciously held beliefs.** This is scary, since most of us will do anything to claw for our status quo, to keep the old guard, to never say "I'm wrong." But I'm aware that I'm a product of my times, blinded to thinking my era is the most "enlightened," that we have been steeped in a Western theology that cannot give up autonomy and drenched in an Eastern theology that cannot imagine a personal, loving God. We're indoctrinated in certain biases that need to be laid aside to see clearly, no matter how uncomfortable that might be, to live inside the whole picture.

It doesn't mean we never question Him—but that we discover the questions He has for us.

This isn't easy—but that's the problem, isn't it? We never dare to allow God to confront us; we shake a fist too fast. I hope we're willing to really wrestle with Him on these things, to step into His timelessness, or we are truly asking to be less human and not more.

It was only Jesus with his pointed, poignant language that could show us our desperate situation, that could wake us out of our religious reverie and all these watered down games, to see how much we truly need him. And only a God who is really this powerful could fully change us and save us, and nothing less than a cross and a tomb could bring us such Good News.

Jesus said such brutally hard things—but he took them on in himself. He took on hell, the worm, the millstone: the sorrow, the fury. That sort of fierce love is the only kind that could wake us from slumber and galvanize us into the blessed, the pure, the peacemakers, into salt and light and the city on a mountaintop.

Truth without love is condescending.
Love without truth is only pretending.
Love and Truth must walk hand-in-hand.

A Narrow Narrow-Gate Theology

Whenever a fellow Christian brings up the "broad road of destruction"—that is, the single verse that implies most people are going to hell—I have to question this with, you know, the Bible.

Because Matthew 25 tells us a story about these ten bridesmaids preparing for the wedding, and half of them are ready. Which implies that probably half of us are going to make it.

Or in Matthew 3, we learn about the wheat getting separated from the chaff, which implies that the majority of us are going to make it.

So which one are we cherry-picking for our agenda?

Do we only use the narrow gate to scare the hell out of people? What about the bridesmaids, and the wheat, and the sins we tend to neglect, and the stuff about helping the orphans and the foreigners and the poor, and how about the criminal next to Jesus who made it in the last ten seconds of his life?

Like my seminary professors used to say, *There's no content without context.*

Maybe we could actually balance our faith with the same nuance that the Bible offers, because no single verse is meant to support a monopoly-theology. Probably we use these verses for power-plays and self-interest and political platforms, when really the Bible is not a polemical grenade but a story of a God who leaps every distance and breaks every obstacle to love His people. It's why Jesus spoke in stories and not bullet points. It's why Jesus didn't draw charts, but he drew people.

There is plenty of hard straightforward truth in the Bible, but without the weaving silver thread of grace, then all our doctrine is a barrel of excuses to dominate each other—and this is exactly what Jesus came to kill and was killed for.

When Jesus talked about a narrow gate, at the very least, he must've known we're always tempted for the easiest path of least resistance, that broad road of incremental choices to nowhere. So he calls himself the Door. He is also a Shepherd, a Mother Hen, a Rock, the Greater Abraham, a Friend, a Fountain, and the King. Each of these pictures give weight and clues and glimpses to who he is, but by themselves, are incomplete. Together, they are just a blink of his glory and beauty. And I'm okay with breathing in the mystery of such infinite truth.

Once in a while, I'll meet someone with a lot of tattoos or a ton of piercings or who curses a lot, and when they find out I'm a Christian, they suddenly apologize for their demeanor and try to cover up. I always feel terrible and then I have to apologize just as quickly—because I don't ever want anyone to feel pre-judged around me.

But that's often how Christians are seen. We judge, condescend, categorize, divide, bicker, and moralize. This is the message we give the most, and it really breaks my heart. I wish new people would feel the most comfortable and safe near me, like they did with Jesus. When someone says, "I knew you were a Christian," I'm always hoping that's a good thing.

A Faith for Yourself

In the middle of the sermon, the pastor said, "You don't need me. You don't need a preacher to tell you what the Bible says. Thank God for scholars and seminaries, but there's no secret insider information. It's all here. You can open up this book and have a faith for yourself."

This wasn't a new thought—but I absolutely appreciated the bald honesty, and I considered how alarmingly dependent we've become on forming our faith and philosophy from others. We wait for Sundays or the right celebrities or our circle of like-minded bloggers to affirm a kind of pre-established dogma, but don't often investigate their words down to the bottom. And they're just people, too, learning like me and you.

I'm not always silent before God to really discern why I believe a certain idea. I run to blogs and books and podcasts too quickly. I try to transplant what works for someone else on to myself, and it doesn't work, and I beat myself up for failing. Other times I'll blame a church or pastor or my community because I trusted them to grow me better, when it was really up to me to learn how to fish. I pride myself on being a "thinker," but too many times I've subconsciously let others do the thinking for me. I trick myself into thinking that having a "click" moment in a sermon is the same thing as real passion and action. I'm very hasty to wonder what someone else thinks about the most recent headlines.

These can only be supplements to the road we must travel ourselves, and we cannot sustain the entire weight of our faith and life and philosophy on other minds who have a road of their own.

You can have a faith for yourself. You don't need me or an articulate witty blogger or someone who has the secret sauce to a better-life-in-seven-easy-steps. There are no shortcuts. There aren't enough words out there to get you where you need to go. Most of the journey is up to you, and me, and each of us in community doing our part.

Don't trust me. There's only One you can truly trust, and He will light the way as we trust Him together.

If you try to make someone do something, you will crush them with expectations. Not even God does that. People need to decide for themselves what to do, without coercion or shaming or manipulation, or else they're only doing it to get you quiet. They won't ever know why, and it will never become a part of them.

Making demands is an external apparatus that will suffocate the people you claim to love. But if you truly love them, by listening and investing and sharing and even liking them, this is the only sort of love that will tenderize a heart to seek better for itself. This is true empowerment.

If words were wounds
and you could see flesh tearing —
would we still speak the same way
or find new ways to destroy ..?
If words were healing
and you could see wounds sealing —
would we still speak the same way
or withhold words to destroy ..?
But this is what it is, every day.
Words rip, words mend —
deeper than flesh, more than metal.
Flesh is fragile,
but a soul, eternal.
Will we still speak the same way?

Instant Replay

I was angry at my friend once for screwing up his life and I sent him an email with a fuming tirade. I was right, I suppose, that sort of right where I had a surge of superiority coursing through my bowels, but the email was so brash and arrogant, I probably wouldn't listen to it, either.

My friend wanted to meet for lunch to seriously discuss how he could get better. He had copied and pasted my entire email into a document and printed it out—and he read it to me over Chinese food and chopsticks. He didn't do it to be hurtful or anything else. He genuinely wanted to clarify my words. We went through it line by awful line.

I was thoroughly embarrassed. To hear myself say those things made me sick to my stomach. Maybe my friend was wrong and I was right, but there's a way to be right without being *right*, when the words are too loud for the intent. It's not enough to be speak truly. Heat only works with light.

I see love in your words,
but I want to hear love in your voice.
Pretty poetry does nothing for me here,
in the dirt, in the earth, at my worst.
Love will cost you more than a pen in motion.
Love means sleeves rolled, hands open, to close in.

Passionately Compassionate: Heart and Fury

When I hear a really loud, fiery, passionate preacher, I want to understand his enthusiasm. But I also wonder if he's in the trenches, serving really messed up people, going to uncomfortable places and loving the weary. If he is—I don't know if he'd still preach like that.

I forget this a lot, too. I forget who I'm talking to.

When I practice my sermons, I sometimes pull up a chair right in front of me.

I picture the fifteen-year-old kid whose parents are divorced and who wants to kill himself everyday and hates everyone at school.

I picture the single mom who lost custody of her children because she can't hold down a job in this economy and drinks herself to sleep every night.

I picture the hard-hearted religious hypocrite who sings loudly every Sunday at his church but goes home to take it out on his kids.

I think of my wife, my future children, I think of the historical figures in the Bible sitting there hearing my preaching.

It's great to sound passionate. But what does real passion sound like?

It sounds like a man nailed to a cross whispering forgiveness over his own murderers. It sounds like a man raised to life calling for the disciple who betrayed him so he could reinstate him back to fruitful ministry. It sounds like Jesus weeping over Jerusalem, angry at a temple for turning God's house into a consumer's playground, raising a young girl to life with the words, "It's time to wake up now, honey."

I'm fine with loud preaching, but what are we loud about?

Injustice requires our outrage and compassion.
Outrage for the wound,
compassion for the wounded.
We do both.

There's a time to say enough is enough. There's a time to vent, weep, scream, shake a fist, and to simply be mad. There's a space when things aren't okay and the injustice is still a fresh wound and no one is supposed to tell you how to feel. We need to grieve before jumping to commentary and those extra little points of debate and platforms and policy. We need to grasp the magnitude of what happened without rushing to a better place, so we can do the hard work of healing deeply, and to ensure that justice is not forfeited for the sake of politeness. Sometimes love has to be outraged, because it won't sit down and take anymore of this. Sometimes love has to get up and fight.

Walking away from an abusive person can be the most gracious thing you could do for them.

Withholding money or resources or your time can be the only way to love that person.

Rebuke is so often exactly what's needed. They have never known the beautiful kiss of discipline. They've never felt the healing power of straightforward truth. They've never known guidance and correction.

We can keep the door wide open. Our arms are ready to embrace. We don't see in black-and-white. Everyone has their side of the story, a right to explain. But those same rights apply to you. You need your own space and room to breathe. We can recover, as long as it takes, before we're back in the fray.

A Chance to Explain

Shortly after I became a Christian, I made a list of every person I had ever wronged and I began calling them to apologize.

The first ring was the worst. My stomach was blowing up and I was ready to get blasted. I heard, "Who's this?"—and like a deranged telemarketer, I quickly stated the purpose of my call and explained my whole pitch, and then I closed by asking, "Can you forgive me?"

"Sure," she said. "Sure, I can."

It was exhilarating. I rushed through the list, my apology gaining polish with every ring.

Finally, my entire enterprise got uppercut dead in its tracks. "No," she said. "You don't get to do this. I'm not some name on a list. I'm not your catharsis."

I was startled out of my game-plan. *Was I doing this for them, or for me?* She went on to say, "Saying sorry doesn't mean you get to explain yourself. It means I get to explain how much what you did actually hurt me."

She was right. I was offloading regret instead of truly *becoming the other*. I was prioritizing my epiphany over their pain. I wasn't the hero here. The hero is the one who makes the call to forgive. I was the bad guy this time, and there was nothing to do but say I was sorry, without excuses, and seeing names as real faces.

It's unfair to rush someone into forgiveness. It's powerful and necessary, but forgiveness isn't a one-time moment that magically seals up the wound. It takes a deliberate, daily battle over a lifetime.

That occasional angry twitch doesn't mean you've failed at finding peace; it's only part of the process, and ignoring it could be worse. The hurt was very real, because it meant something. That's no excuse to hold a grudge for long, but no one is allowed to rush your healing, including you. No one can just "get over it." But I do hope to see you on the other side, where there's freedom. You can take all the time you need, and I'm with you.

It's so strange: there was a person I had a really hard time forgiving, but I loved on him so much in public and only talked good about him behind his back that I sort of came to like him, and in the meantime, forgive him without hardly knowing. Our words are so powerful, they can direct the entire course of the heart who speaks them.

A Road To Converge:
Letting Go of the Pain You're Passing On

I had a friend who was dating a girl, and the girl eventually left him for his boss. They had to work together. I can't imagine how hard it must have been.

Years later, my friend opened his own business, but he took all his hurts with him. He hardly opened up to anyone, viciously arm-wrestled for authority, shut off anyone he didn't trust, boiled hate at meetings, and ran his business under a strict disciplinary cage. Some said this was always his personality—but I knew him from before. His once infectious playfulness had turned into a passive-aggressive moodiness and cold distance.

We parted ways long ago; I no longer met his invisible standard. I was upset, but the more I thought about it, the more I understood. If I had gone through the same thing, I might have carried over all that baggage, too.

The hard truth is that the trauma and trials that we go through are not the worst things that can happen to us. The worst is *when we give it permission to define us by a toxic lie*—that somehow the world is bereft of any good, that we never have to trust again, that we can retaliate first, that we owe others bitterness and contempt. The worst is when we rehearse our own sad story to the point where even the future is to blame, and every new face must pass a test designed to fail. It is a harsh whisper in your heart that says, "Never again. I'll show *them*."

All of this is understandable. I'm on your side about that. *But this constant sour whisper will slowly destroy you.* It will destroy everything you touch. I know this because I lost a great friend to it, and I've lost myself to it before, too. My friend refuses to acknowledge what's happening, and it hurts my heart to see him stomp his way through life with closed fists. It hurts to see him interpret all disagreement as opposition, or to assume the most innocuous interactions are a call to war. I miss the person that he once was and could still be.

I know why we can get this way, *but I grieve for those who define their lives by the losses they have incurred.* You may have been embarrassed, stabbed in the back, betrayed, and cheated—no one's saying it isn't wrong, no one's saying that forgiveness must come quickly or easily—but it's even *more reason* to find recovery and peace, or else you will not pass on wisdom, but pain.

I know it hurts. Maybe life has not gone the way you wanted, and of course, there is room to grieve. I can only pray that it will be one part of the whole and not the entire journey. There is time yet to re-route, to pave a new way. Perhaps our roads will converge one day again.

Repentance is not just a one-time turn around, but a thousand small daily deaths to yourself. It's living for the one whom you were saved by to do what you were made for. It's not merely saying no to something, but saying yes to the best thing.

Hold You True to You

If you're only surrounded by yes-men, you'll drive off every cliff. You'll be out of touch with reality. You'll drift into complacency and you won't grow. If this makes you mad or uncomfortable: you might already be heading that way.

We've seen this happen a million times. Someone never got the hard talk, so they became their own boss and got blindsided by a blind spot. Someone only befriended like-minded people, and was isolated in conspiratorial agreement. Someone never heard the hard truth, and they were shrunk into a feeble shadow of their potential.

I'm not talking about someone else. It's for you. It's for me. We need the hard talk once in a while, to shake the cobwebs.

We need someone to hold up the mirror to hold us accountable, to say even with a shaking voice, "You're better than this."

I don't mean that we become the morality-police for every infraction. It's tougher, and better. A friend brings another perspective, another point of reference, another angle, another voice, to round us out, to stretch us. It can be enough to sober us up. When we get out of character, we need someone who brings us back. We need to be held true to the person we were always meant to be.

Power-Drunk Judgment

Accountability is necessary, but it can also get danger-ous. The danger is that when you're given the responsibil-ity to constructively criticize or to call someone out, it's easy to start looking for little things like it's your job. The filter can get so tight that it becomes more about prefer-ence than promoting growth, and it gets abused.

Years ago, I had an accountability partner who went drunk with critical power-madness. He saw more and more negative in me until I could hardly do anything without some remark over the sinful implications of my actions. He thought he was "being honest" and being "deep." And I went the other way: I was less and less willing to call him out on anything because I wanted to play nice. It would only look like I was fighting back. I neglected his spiritual growth because I was so reluctant to get into a back-and-forth tango over what amounted to legalistic minutiae. I became paranoid, fearful, silent. He grew shrill and resent-ful. I dreaded our time together. The friendship fell apart.

Accountability can only come from the momentum of an established friendship, when it's a part of the whole package of joy and laughter and even doing nothing. To specifically label "accountability partners" for the sole purpose of straightening each other out is a time-bomb. We either judge too much or let each other off the hook. Love is a fire that must burn without burning one another.

Often the best theology your friend needs right now is you. Not more lectures or advice. You're the miracle they're praying for.

Honesty is the first step to healing. It's only with a surgical self-confrontation that you can be liberated from the lies you have believed. You can see the lie for what it really is. It's only by stepping back from the momentum of darkness that has swallowed up your vision will you begin to see once more. The light is staggering, blinding, even humiliating, but to see yourself as you really are is to begin the path to be set free.

No one wants to hear the truth about themselves—but if you deny any lies about your own life, it will control you for the rest of your life. It's when we know we are blind that we first truly see.

Leave the Old, Breathe in the New

There's an ancient Greek word, *ouketi*, which means, "No longer." The word is often used as, "I'm no longer who I was before." It's a sweeping decision to move forward into something new. It starts with knowing you cannot live as you were.

If you really want to do the thing, it requires cutting off a few things. I know that no one wants to hear about it, because it sounds like I'm telling you what to do. I get that. I hate it too. We naturally push back against authority. We're individualistic creatures who want total autonomy—but autonomy is a process of depositing your choices in the right places in a consecutive momentum, so that later, you will have the unhindered ability to live the life you actually wanted. It's like learning the notes on a keyboard, at first clumsy and restricted, but later being able to play the most beautiful of compositions and even making your own. We invest our first choices in the soil so that we may bloom for better choices in the sun.

It's not a one-time decision. It means saying *ouketi* each and every day. Some days, it'll feel like you've moved only an inch. You'll relapse sometimes. You'll be tempted to go back. But inch by inch, you'll have moved miles without hardly knowing it. You will look back on those old things and wonder how you got so wrapped up in them. You'll look into a future that you'll finally be excited for.

Created for Adventure Above

Humans were created for adventure, story, a mission, a purpose. It's why we'll pay to watch someone else's made-up life on a giant screen in a dark room with other strangers. We crave the unfolding narrative of good conquering evil and the rejected finding love. We yearn to be part of something bigger than ourselves.

But when we float aimlessly in limbo, without a better truth, we'll inevitably latch onto smaller selfish drama. It's in our nature to find action somewhere, and when it's not food, it's poison. If it's not real, it'll be the cheap imitation. We'll puff up the petty stuff to fit that hunger. We'll end up investing our emotions into trivial, trashy, inconsequential things. We'll get caught up in workplace conflicts and gossip loops and grudges over words we can't remember. We'll find "love" in the nearest face, driven by the surface high of meeting new people while avoiding the deeper work of getting to know them, and ourselves. We'll focus on the little harmless quirks in someone that irritate us, like a look they make or the way they talk, and unfairly exaggerate those tiny inconveniences. We'll hijack someone else's very real pain for our own platforms, as if fighting for a "real cause," when it's really just prideful snobbery at the sound of our own voices — all while neglecting the actual offense. We'll make everything a big deal, when not everything deserves the same amount of time and energy and space in our minds.

You're going to find drama somewhere. We're already investing in it, a breath at a time. It's a matter of which story we choose to tell. I hope we'll make it a good one.

You don't owe anyone an explanation.
You're not required to defend your passion.
But you owe it to yourself
to know what you're really about.

What Breaks My Heart
Is When You Don't Hear Mine

I've always had trouble approaching someone with a fragile ego, because I know if I say anything disagreeable or honest, they'll defend themselves like crazy with a million excuses or throw insults or throw things off the desk or make ugly-cry-face and cut me off for a month.

Everyone knows the guy who *can't* handle rebuke—it's like walking on egg shells over thin ice over a mine-field—and if you dare bring up a hint of contradiction, they will either melt down or throw things or suck you into a terrible black hole.

You know the guy who knows what's best for everyone, but the moment you bring up a suggestion, it's sniped down from a throne-room in a walled-up fortress. I've had friends like this, who became defensive and sensitive to correction but continued to trample others with hands on both ears.

I know all this because I was that guy, too. It was only when I began to listen to others' concerns, to receive rebuke as life, that I could quit the fear of being challenged into change.

Without rebuke, we're left sauntering in an unseen cloud of darkness that threatens to destroy us by a gradual downhill fade. The most dangerous way to die is slowly, unaware, in descent.

A few years ago, one of my best friends was messing up with something. No one else knew but me. It probably wasn't a big deal, and no one would've been hurt if he continued, but I had to bring it up. I really didn't want to, but I couldn't just sit by.

My friend is the coolest guy in the world. I've never seen him rage out or say a harsh word in his life. He was the kind of guy who walked away from a group the second they began to gossip, who didn't hesitate to break up a street fight on his way home.

But even when I bring the truth to the coolest people, I've seen the worst come out of them. There's always a mirror-defense where they decide to bring up *your* grievances, or a lot of casual dismissal, or loud, angry hostility. I was so jaded by this sort of thing that I didn't expect much different here, either.

On a Friday, we were at my place and I sat him down and started with the ominous statement, "I have to talk to you about something." My voice shook for that entire sentence. If I wasn't sitting down, my knees probably would've been shaking too.

I told him everything. I said, "I don't want anyone else to say something bad about you, that's why I'm saying this. You're my friend, you're my brother, I want the best for you."

After I was done, I braced myself. I physically reeled back, waiting for the shouting match.

My friend said, "Thank you"—and then he stood up without a word and went to the door, and he left.

For some reason, this was *worse*. I couldn't sleep that night. I thought I had totally screwed this up. Friendship, ruined. Years of loyalty, over. I kept going over what I said in my brain, all the ways I should've worded it differently.

The next day, my friend came by. He sat me down, the same place, the same chairs. He said, "I thought about what you said. And you're right. I'm going to stop immediately."

My entire body unclenched. To be truthful, I almost wept. I hate to cry in front of people, but I was just so dang relieved. Some of it was because I was emotionally tightened up, and some of it was my anxiety that I was no longer his friend. But mostly I couldn't believe that *another human being actually considered what I said and thought it was the best course of action, so he changed his life over it*. I was astonished.

It would've been okay if he cussed me out, or never spoke to me again, or kept living his life as before. I would've understood. I would've loved him the same.

No one owes me anything, and this is not about him "following me." But the plot-twist is that he actually listened. Not to me, but to *wisdom*. I can't remember a time when it happened so quickly, so graciously.

He stuck to his word. He stopped. He went out of his way to make sure it never happened again. And I never said "I told you so," or "It's better now right?" or "Aren't you glad you listened?" If anything, we grew closer and stronger. I was one of the groomsmen for his wedding and he was a groomsman for mine.

Even in the best of friendships, rebuke is a risk, and if you ever get to that place of honesty, there will be a space of tension where the friendship hangs in the balance. There will be an initial emotional reaction. There will be sorts of frantic excuses and attacks. And I hope you can push past this. I hope you don't take it too personally. Every creature has an instinct of self-defense. The only thing we can do is to endure the scratching and stumble through those first reactions, and maybe we can move past this part a little quicker each time.

I hope we can pursue rebuke, to pursue truth, for spiritual surgery. I hope you can run through my overreactions and get to that core inside, where you believe I can do better, and you sincerely do love me. I hope you will hear my heart breaking.

I Will, Anyway

In the end, you can't really force someone to do anything, even if it's for their good.

You can't force someone to respect your feelings or care about your passions or believe your dreams.

You can't force someone to believe your side of the story, even when you're right.

You can't force an apology.

You can't force someone to engage in justice or fight for the poor or to become nuanced in culture and history.

You can't force growth.

You can't force someone to show up ∂n time, or even show up at all.

In the end, I've learned that people will do whatever they want, even if that means stepping on you or neglecting you or abandoning you or belittling you or choosing others over you. I've probably done this as much as it's been done to me. It's a terrible cycle that leaves us bitter, suspicious, paranoid, and completely jaded.

I've also learned that I don't care if you don't care. I have to love anyway. I have to be patient anyway. I have to be jaded to being jaded. Because I don't want to perpetuate someone else's cycle of apathy and neglect. I don't want to be one more rung in the ladder of indifference. I don't want to be a reactionary pawn.

No, I cannot force anything on you, and I won't. I can only pour out what I have. Even if you don't care. Especially if you don't care. I'll pour out anyway. In the end, our lives will have been given over to dust. I'd rather mine will have been given over to you.

"Let us hold unswervingly to the hope we profess,
for he who promised is faithful.
And let us consider
how we may spur one another on
toward love and good deeds.
Let us not give up meeting together,
as some are in the habit of doing,
but let us encourage one another —
and all the more as you see the Day approaching."
— Hebrews 10:23-25

"Search me, O God,
and know my heart;
test me and know my anxious thoughts.
See if there is any offensive way in me,
and lead me in the way everlasting."
— Psalm 139:23-24

You, Too?
Me, Too

Sometimes I forget to listen. I forget to let a friend *be*. To tell their whole story and paint their full heart into the air.

I'm too eager to respond with a fix, a solution, a plan. I interrupt the art. I look for a pause to jump in and offer all sorts of articulate banter, when this isn't what they want. They just want to speak until they're out of breath, and then meet eyes and feel like they're okay and understood and not alone. It's a beautiful thing, and I want to let it happen. I want to let them finish painting in their own words. And then maybe I will understand.

At times I'm afraid you'll see right through me, into the dark, and you'll run screaming.

I'm afraid you'll get to know me, and I won't be as impressive as the hologram I have put on.

I'm scared you'll see me as I really am, the dirty scarred horrible ugly kid inside, the irredeemable veiny creature beneath the hand-shaking smiles I wear all day.

I can only remember that I saw the darkest of you, too, and it did not scare me, but rather drew me in, because I could not help but traverse the contours of your jagged heart. I tasted the worst of you, the fits and flailing and slobbery angry rage, but I also saw in you the very best, the passion to do good and to fight for you true self. None of this because of what you had yet to do, but because your wounds were your beauty, and your scarred heart was a story I wanted to discover.

You saw through me, yet drew closer still. We sculpted our journey, the mountains and valleys, together. We are fellow travelers, always.

I can't judge someone based on a tweet, a picture, a blog post, or 0.001% of their entire life on display. I won't.

We're often seeing a person on the way to who they want to be. It's rife with misinformed opinions and unsound logic and lapses in common sense. I've been the idiot, too.

That person you call a hypocrite might just be someone on the first lap of their faith, still wrestling with the old life.

Even if someone should know better, so should I, about something that I haven't seen yet. I want to give a fair chance, because I was given so many, and it was understanding that brought me here so far.

Intimacy, Wounds, Trust, Horizon

Occasionally we let someone in, we open the folds of our insecurity and give access to the darkest parts of us. We hand over the key, and it's terrifying. And sometimes they bump into a raw nerve, they say a callous insensitive remark, they ridicule a strange notion we have, they poke at our dreams just a bit. It hurts pretty bad and we push them out and fold up fast. We remind ourselves, "This is why I don't let anyone in." And we run.

It's right here that most people apologize like crazy. They feel terrible. They were trying to figure out how to navigate the labyrinth of your wonderful story. It's like holding a tiny flash light in a cave of a new world. They didn't mean to provoke those old wounds. They didn't mean to poke fun at your dreams. They considered it an honor that they held the key, even for a few frenzied moments.

Intimacy takes work, trust, wounds, hurts, sculpting in the dark: and that takes time. It takes more than a single chance. Of course we can close the doors, at any second, when we know it just won't work. But there are many opportunities if we had trusted a little longer, reset the tempo, and spoke up louder: it would've been okay. Bridges would be built. New stories are made. You find your hand closing around theirs. They begin to traverse the folds of your heart with ease, and they learn to say those things which give life, which give freedom, which grow dreams. Intimacy is formed out of stumbling, but further down the path, there is so much light, so much laughter, so many steps to the horizon together.

As I was leaving church the other week, a little Sunday School kid said, "I won't be here this Sunday. Can you give me a hug? And can you remember my name?" Suddenly I knew what Jesus felt like when he picked up children with their arms wide open, and I'm reminded of every human desire: to be known by name, and to be embraced. It's the heart of a kid who doesn't want to be forgotten.

A Secret World of Sinners

When I first came to church, I thought all the Christians there were naive, susceptible, weak-minded overly protected religious people who didn't know the harsh underside of life.

But the more I got to know them, the more I heard their hard stories of heartbreak and secret addictions and sleepless regrets. I found they were naturally prideful and stubborn and had every reason to hate God—just like me.

I had really judged too quickly. I was seeing many of them on the other side of this process called transformation. No one there was the one-dimensional sketch I had imagined them to be. And no one—including me—were arriving to a put-together faith. They were beat up and clinging to Christ. Jesus loved them, and even liked them: these weary, sin-torn, ragged individuals who longed for healing. And I discovered that I fit right in.

I ended up liking Jesus, too.

There are friendships I've mourned over where too much history got in the way. There were too many harsh words and broken promises and silent disagreements, and it rotted to an impatient grave.

But there are others where we traveled the jagged road of reconciliation, mending wounds and untying knots and covering with grace: and on the other end of this is an ocean-deep intimacy of perseverance that couldn't be reached any other way. We had to wrestle with the ugly parts of our nature. Demons were exposed. Secrets were spilled.

Yet there is a joy in this sort of enduring friendship that goes the long distance; there's a crazy sort of laughter with a lifelong friend that is colored by the weight of heels digging into the ground, a love that says, "I'm staying." We see it in the cross, and we can have it now, even in a world such as this.

I Rejected Jesus

At a gas station, a young brother asked me for ten dollars. He needed a pair of shoes to start his new job at a fast food joint or they would tell him to go home on his first day. He said, "I'm just stepping out in faith, man. Please."

These kinds of things happen in town all the time. Addicts and the homeless begging for coins, single mothers asking for gas money. As a reflex, I said no. He thanked me and walked off defeated. I suddenly remembered: I had exactly ten dollars in my wallet.

I should've stopped him, but I didn't. I drove off and spent the ten dollars on something probably much less important. I hoped maybe someone else gave him ten dollars. Maybe his manager gave him a break. Maybe he was lying. Maybe he would've spent it on drugs. Maybe.

I know one thing for sure. I turned down Jesus that day. I remembered Matthew 25:40—

"I tell you the truth, whatever you did for one of the least of these brothers of mine, you did for me."

Whether this guy would do the right thing with the money, I know I did not. For every crowd-pleasing story I could tell you, most of them really end up like this one, regretful over a ten dollar bill that was worth eternity.

I'm sorry, young brother. I beg of your forgiveness. Next time the shoes are on me. And I'll tell you about the one who will wash your feet, the same one who washed mine, too.

I think there are some of us who are pouring out so much and working so hard and giving so much to others that we're entirely spent and don't even know it. It's a hidden debilitation that we ended up just living with and becoming blind to, a bleeding hole in your back. We sort of forget what it's like to have time to ourselves and simply revel in life. I hope you can wake from that sort of slumber, even for a moment, to smell the day again.

Rush In, a Shoulder to Spare

The toughest thing is to see a person you love get to the edge of their resolve and quietly fall apart. It's a slumping of the shoulders or a long hurtful sigh or a sarcastic remark or they blink away a tear. It's different than hysterics. There's a silent internal folding like a shot in the gut, a hollow feeling of resigned pointlessness: and it's so deadly quiet.

In that moment, they may be too embarrassed to ask for help or to expose how weak they really feel. But I hope it's that exact moment we rush in to hold them up. I hope we fill up that crumpled collapsed space with a word of life. To remind them of their value, worth, dignity, to show the progress they have made up this mountain.

I hope we don't simply plod along when we know there's something wrong, but we fly in there with the audacity to rebel against their resignation, as gentle as a surgeon and until our voice shakes.

It won't be pretty. Probably it'll feel like you're not even helping. Real love is gritty, messy, clumsy, unpolished, raw. It's not at all romantic or like a scripted Hollywood epiphany.

But our words do not need to be witty or wise or altogether right. We just need someone to fall on, to lift our heavy arms, to be close enough to feel our hot tired breath: even for one more step. And to be that for someone reminds us why we do anything at all. We remember that the fabric of life is together, a journey of side-by-side, so that even a failure is not the end of anything, but only a deepening of you and me.

We're With You Up There

I took a speech class in college because of my stage fright, and the professor, Mr. Johns, was about the most encouraging guy on the face of the earth.

There was a girl in the class who was just like me, taking the class because she wanted to overcome her fear. In her first speech, she burst into tears and couldn't stop shaking. I thought I had it bad, but this girl came undone at the seams. I was worried that we'd have to call an ambulance for her. She wanted to stop but the professor got up right next to her, nudging her to finish. Some of the others stood with her and we cheered her on, rooting for her, clapping and fist-pumping and even saying "amen" the whole way. She finished the speech. By her final one, she could do it up front by herself. She knew we were still with her up there.

One of the reasons I'm so intensely insecure and self-conscious is because everyone keeps talking about "be yourself"—but the moment you open up, you're only accepted when "being yourself" is a certain type of self. It's really romantic that we push a magical version of vulnerable and unique, but the actual opening up part is dang hard and uncomfortable and requires a kind of love that most people won't muster, since they've never really had to. It ain't like Hollywood, ever.

If you find the sort of friend who truly loves you, I mean the weird obnoxious squeaky sweaty you, however imperfectly, keep them close and forgive them for when they do not understand. Friendship will take more than once and more than the pretty picture in our heads.

Everyone loves the idea of compassion until it costs them. We love the idea of love until it comes to "unlovable" people. We think a romantic programmatic workshop of willing people: but it's actually messy, difficult, heartbreaking, and requires your whole life.

What they also don't tell you is that it's awesome. When you're face to face, chair to chair, eye to eye with a real person, there's nothing like seeing the lights go on, the lies disentangled, the burden lifted, the problems exposed, the trauma healed, the heart rejoicing—there is absolutely nothing that compares to the pinnacle of God's glory in one human being discipling another. I mean really discipling them, to just love someone. That click you hear is the something-missing being filled. To love people is what you're created to do. Once you get there, you can't go back anymore.

Jealousy: A World Held Back

My friend was telling me about this really good preacher, and immediately I tried to play "gotcha" with the preacher's theology, to poke holes in the sermon, to conclude some evil character flaw. It was so automatic I felt the criticism go up my throat like acid reflux.

I managed to catch myself. *Why so jealous?* What if the preacher was actually bad? Would I have been happy about that? Because part of me thinks that yes, I would've been thrilled.

Suddenly the truth bubbled up through my conscience: *I'm scared when someone is better than me.*

It was violently disorienting. I felt sick to stomach. Finally I forced my mouth to say, "I'm really glad you were moved by the sermon." The words barely made it through my clenched, contorted teeth as I seethed it through pursed lips.

Why was it so hard to compliment this preacher I've never met before?

I've probably done this hundreds of times. We quickly and casually dismiss someone's God-given potential by finding the tiniest crack in their ability—and of course, if we look hard enough, we'll find something. It will somehow make us feel okay again, because we're always threatened by someone who is slightly better than ourselves.

A friend will share someone else's work with me, a blog post or song or video or charity—and sometimes I'll throw a smug, suffocating filter on their creation until I mentally strangle them into a worthless heap. I'll bring a friend to the gym and he'll say, "Look at that guy, he ain't even that big." Or at work, I'll hear, "He has it easy. She has everything handed to her."

We all know the guy who constantly finds problems with someone. "I like this guy, *but* the thing is ..." or "Yeah he was good, *but* my problem with him is ..."

I hate seeing this. I hate doing this. And this catty game of competition is exhausting.

I know we have the right to criticize. We must discern when something is off. But rarely do I witness true celebration over someone's hard work. I mostly see a witch hunt for weaknesses, to nitpick and diminish until we find a horrible satisfaction with someone's downfall.

I have to move against myself on this and get out of my own way. Otherwise, I fail to pass on the torch and I hold back an entire world of people because of our petty insecurities. We write off those with potential and prevent our own growth by not learning from those who have surpassed us. And I'm not growing an empire. I want to grow gardens.

Be passionate for your friend's passion.

You don't have to get it,

but you don't have to bash it, either.

If it's important to them, it's important to you, too.

Where You Can Be You

One value I cherish more than almost any other is honesty. I mean being vulnerable. We can put on a good front out there but this slowly strangles us inside, and it's probably why the world is the way that it is: because we've bottled up everything about us inside tiny cubicles of courtesy, a tightly coiled parade of modified bravado.

I heard a theory once that conspiracy theories could not exist, because the people hiding those elaborate lies would just blow up. No one's good at keeping secrets too long, most especially our own. We need a safe place to deposit them somewhere, to not be judged for them, to know our tears and scars are not wasted in the silent echo of hiding, to say, "I'm not okay right now."

I think we need that one friend who's an open-and-shut vault, where we can vent and just go nuts. You know, the one friend where we can be our slobbery, screwed up, frustrated, upside-down selves. And they still hang around in the morning because that's what love does: it says good morning. It sticks around.

A culture of honesty could only come from a culture of grace, where we have the undeserved hope of being known but still loved. We crave honesty. You have a friend like that: don't ever let that go. They see you at your darkest and limp with you to the light.

A Moment of Real Life for Life

I once met up someone who had found me on my blog and he happened to live in the same town.

I get really anxious about this sort of thing and I usually say no, because I feel like my blog is a trailer for a movie that will inevitably let you down. I don't think I'm very impressive in real life, and people have a way of hyping things up in their head. Anything less is like seeing a painting up close: the *Mona Lisa* is really small and dinky, if you ever seen it, and I ain't no Mona Lisa.

This guy was really persistent though, and why not?—he lived right down the street. We met at Starbucks and he had brought along a few of his friends. We got to cracking jokes and sharing stories and it was all going pretty well. We stayed an hour and it was a good time.

The guy never reached out again. He never posted the pictures we took. He went ghost on my social media.

I wasn't sure if I had said something wrong, and I kept replaying it all. But I think I understood, too. Not everyone is meant to be lifelong friends. Not everyone decides to follow up. I have to respect those reasons, and that can't always be indicative of what went right or wrong. I suppose I was glad to be there for an hour of laughter, even if there was none after. Paintings last for a moment, and I was okay to be that for a day.

Drive-By Witness

Once someone took me out to lunch and really took an interest in the drama I was going through. He listened, nodded, encouraged, and even prayed.

But then I never heard from him again.

Then I later discovered —

1) He was only curious about the latest gossip in town, 2) he felt like hanging out once was his good-enough deed for the day, and 3) he did it to impress me and puff up his own ego.

It's a bit heartbreaking because —

1) I really thought he cared, 2) I was excited to have someone who could walk through my stuff, and 3) it's so hard to find trustworthy friends these days.

Of course, this didn't stop me from opening up to others, and I'm always willing to risk the chance.

I just don't want to be a drive-by witness. People are not hotel rooms; you can't just check in and check out. If we're going to be there, then I hope we'd *be there*. And really care.

Life Is Interruption: Take the Detour

There was this one Sunday when I totally bombed the sermon. I mean, I have hits and misses, home runs and off-days, like everyone else—but this particular Sunday left me in a self-condemning daze.

I had prepared like crazy but we had just switched buildings, so there was no sound system, no air conditioner, and a noisy hallway with heads popping in. My thoughts never gelled together and the sermon failed to find a rhythm. About five minutes in, I knew that everyone was checking out.

When the whole thing became unbearable, I cut the sermon short by ending with a metaphor and a story. For a second everyone listened, and they seemed grateful I had enough sense to end early. At the very least, I was able to land the plane.

I discovered that I was actually less upset about the sermon itself, but more about having to adapt to the room. I get easily irritated when "my plans," whether for a sermon or alone-time or date-night, get foiled by an unexpected turn of events. And really, most of our well-laid plans will get interrupted by inconveniences. Nothing unfolds the way we picture it in our head. There's no ideal room or perfectly isolated space where perfect magic can happen.

It's during these escalated, frustrating times that we need to think on our feet and be flexible enough to serve the reality of the room. That meant that I had to pay more attention to the people around me instead of just mindlessly marching through with my agenda. It meant I couldn't unroll everything I had prepared, that all my careful research and prayer and prep was getting shafted, that I couldn't function at my best. I could only make some good out of a bad situation.

But that's okay. I think these moments are necessary to humble us towards the needs of others, to be sensitive to what's happening. I don't think we need to get everything right in a day. I think I needed to learn how to serve others in that icky, sweaty, gritty sort of setting, because life is not like the movies where the temperature is always perfect and we get our Hollywood halftime-speech moment and the day wraps up with a pretty bowtie. Life gets amusing and raw and slippery, and I want enough sense to laugh about that. We can meet each other there. And of course, there's always next week.

Turning an Endless Jewel

I've found that everyone's Christian faith is utterly, uniquely different. Not so different on loving Jesus and loving people — but the way we wrestle through doctrine by strict academia or by poetic reflection, how we sing at the top of our lungs or in quiet osmosis, how some of us pray at sunrise in a pew or at three a.m. on a beach, how some of us are dying to journal or would rather die than journal, how our political tensions clash so broadly and brutally, how one forgives so quickly and the other is bitter indefinitely, how some of us are strong in faith or we're faith-weaklings, how we each hold onto quirks like Bible translations and worship genres and preaching styles, how we like to gather in crowds of thousands or a group of a dozen.

There's no need to fight over these things. No need to accuse another of being wrong, or to try to be better than the 'other' church, or to recast the same mold. We are so many shades of an endless jewel, a glorious community of unified diversity fueled by the endless imagination of God. I hope we don't dash ourselves on our personalities. There is room for you and for me in this Body.

The lie is that "doing great things for God" has to look huge like Hollywood. It's possible that you're called to China or to Uganda or to sell all your stuff for charity. That would be awesome. But great things also include: raising your kids, writing a song, greeting on Sundays, listening over coffee, and loving your next-door neighbor. Also awesome.

Stay Encouraged, Gangster Moll

I once lived in an apartment building where I could hear the mother next door raising her kids, and she would play this Barney tape every day. You know the song: "I love you, you love me, we're a happy family," over and over and over. One day, I thought I heard this mother sigh. Like a really long, exasperated sigh. And suddenly I wanted to tell this lady, "Don't do it! Don't run from your kids! Don't move to Vegas and find some rich dude and become some gangster moll!"

She was probably not in danger of doing any of this, and no one says "gangster moll" anymore. But I was worried. Maybe she was checking out. Maybe she felt she was missing another life. Maybe she needed a vacation, too. I had half a mind to go next door and bring a cake or something, but I'd imagine that would be alarming ("I'm the Asian guy next door, also here's a cake I attempted to bake. Don't mind my creeper face."). Thinking back, I probably should've encouraged her somehow. To at least tell her, "It's pretty hard, right?" Because preparation and expectations are half the battle. Perseverance is really hard, but it's not so bad if you know what you're in for, and if you know that you're not alone.

Everyone is way too hard on each other about things we don't fully understand.

When we see someone wearing a cast, we don't hurry them along or force them to health. We do all we can to maneuver their broken bone, to work with them, to cheer for their strength and recovery. All of us wear casts: just not on the outside.

"How Do You Keep Believing In All This Faith S__?"

Often I'll have a friend from childhood find out that I'm a pastor and they're downright incredulous; they're just as surprised as I am that I ever went from atheism to Christianity, much less ministry. "I thought you were too smart for that," or, "You were always the wild guy, I never thought you'd settle down."

Most of my friends went the other way and fell out of faith like it was a varsity jacket, or an old diaper. They ask, "How do you keep believing in all this faith s__?" – not because they're trying to trap me, but because they're genuinely curious for a coherent explanation. They do want something.

To be truthful, most times, I don't have a good answer.

I often wonder the same: *How do I keep believing this faith s__?*

There are these troubling moments that I find the whole thing just crazy. When I reduce Christianity down to one or two sentences, it sounds ridiculous coming out of my mouth. *I believe that if I telepathically offer my cognitive affection to a Jewish zombie who tells us to eat his flesh and drink his blood, then I'll have immortality and half a better chance to run for political office.*

A fellow Christian will tell me, "Oh no, doubt is a good thing, it means you're at the edge of solidifying a deeper faith by investigating your most foundational beliefs." Which I guess could be true.

A fellow atheist will tell me, "Oh no, doubt is a good thing, it means you're at the edge of coming back to reason and shedding a fear-based crutch that's having less relevance and respect in the world." Which I guess could also be true.

Both would say about doubt: "You're finally being intellectually honest." Both say, "You'll come around." Both say, "If those people could just admit they don't have everything right." Both say, "They're just so blind and have the same boring arguments and the 'burden of proof' is on them."

Both can be rude, unthoughtful, unmoving. And of course, they both love to yell *ad hominem.*

It all just sounds the same to me. I could quit believing. I could keep believing. I could walk away. I could walk harder.

Occasionally, I binge-read all the atheist classics again and I spend long nights on atheist blogs trying to beat my faith into submission. I consider the horrors of the world and how I wouldn't trust the sort of God who lets this happen, either. The arguments from the "other side" are compelling and hard to fight, and I remember how comfortable I was in my unbelief, how much easier it was not to scratch for an invisible rope to Heaven.

Why do you keep believing?

I'm not entirely sure all the time. I have long miserable episodes of doubt where I feel tricked, like I somehow had a greater psychological propensity to be duped by some smooth-talking preacher. I wonder if faith is merely sentimental scaffolding that tickles an emotional chord of nostalgia in my artsy inner-child. I wonder if I've bought into a cultural club of insider-acceptance where we all reluctantly agree on the Jesus-stuff because it allows us to have potlucks and socials. I wonder if I'm just a weak-minded wishful thinker and that it's making me more bigoted, more exclusive, more withdrawn and arrogant and smug, than if I simply just left it all behind.

I wish I had a bow-tie to wrap this all up for you. I don't. I wish I had a, "And then I realized —" but I don't. Not always. It's insanely difficult, this believing stuff.

I stand between two cliffs of conflicted opposition, both sides looking for answers and seeking ever deeper, and I think maybe that neither side is so different than the other. I think maybe all of us doubt, and we doubt our doubts, and it will be this way to the end. When I'm asked, "Why do you keep believing?"—I can only say, "Believing is hard. For you, for me, for everyone. But this particular thing, even when I least believe it, I *hope* it would be true. I can tell you all the evidence, but what it *does,* it's a whole universe inside here, man."

Maybe that's a cop-out. I don't know. I just look at the long, twisted road behind me, and I don't miss who I used to be. It could be psychological trickery. It could be cultural dressing. Or maybe there's a whole universe in here, and eternity has made its way in.

Jesus said that faith the size of a mustard seed can move mountains. The hard part is that mountains are so big, and a seed so small, and I feel like David trusting in a tiny stone, wondering if it's enough.

I do want to believe it, though. I want to believe that at some point in human history, a perfect God really did break into the turbulent chaos of our world and reversed our inevitable condition, at one place in time, to bring about a healing from the sky to the grave to our hearts. I want to believe that such a boundary-breaking love can exist, that such a person would know the depth of my ugliness and draw in with his beauty. It's a wonderful, brilliant, heart-gripping story. I hope, by God, that it really is true. I hope against myself. I hope for you.

I've tried to turn away from God so many times. I've tried everything else. I've spent and chased and invested and used. In the end: Where else could I go? Nothing else fulfills me when I find it; nothing else forgives me when I fail it. No one takes me back like He does.

We All Got Through

I imagine that when Moses split the Red Sea, there were two groups of people.

The first group was composed of victorious triumphant warriors saying, "In your face, Egyptians! This is our God!" They were pumping their fists and thrusting their spears. The second group was composed of doubtful, panicking screamers running full speed through whales and plankton.

I'm a Screamer. I'm a cynic. I'm a critic. I'm a Peter, who can make a good start off the boat, but falls in the water when my eyes wander. I'm not endorsing a halfway lukewarm faith. I believe God wants us to have a robust, vibrant, thriving relationship with Him. But as for me, I'll be limping to the finish-line. I'm more of a Thomas than a Paul. I'm more Martha than Mary. I'm more David than Daniel.

Yet the Warriors and Screamers all made it through.

It's not easy to have faith the size of a muslurd seed. But Jesus promised that this would be enough to move mountains, and I'm learning to be okay with that.

Making Prayer Harder Than It Really Is

I don't know *anyone* who thinks they're praying as much as they should.

When the preacher tells us to pray more, we really want to. It's a constant, itchy, burdening debt. Days, weeks, months go by with a handful of failed attempts — and each prayer feels like we're apologizing.

I'm sorry I haven't prayed in so long. I'm sorry it's not longer than a few minutes. I'm sorry it's not "deeper."

Prayer is hard though, if you ever really tried it.

I mean in the first five minutes, you start thinking of other stuff. A lot. *Did I leave the stove on? Should I send that email first? Did I respond to that text? Should I do some sit-ups?* It feels like running through an iron stocking, with all these distractions and interruptions and runaway thought-trains.

Then there's the doubting. We don't know if it's working. Or if God is listening. Or if we're doing it right. Or if we're too dirty to pray. Or if I even need to, since God does what He wants anyway.

There's all these spiritually incriminating moments that make me want to give up.

I've probably said, "I'll pray for you" a billion times, and then just forgot half the time.

I always feel so motivated to pray at church in a big boomy atmosphere with more mature people—but then I feel that guilt accusing me of convenient hypocrisy.

Whenever I pray before a meal, it reminds me how little I pray elsewhere.

When I pray out loud for a group, I'm often grasping for the right words, modifying my own voice to fit the crowd, self-consciously picking Christianese phrases like "bring God the glory" and "rain down mercy" and "holy fire fill us." I don't know what these mean, to tell you the truth.

Can we just admit it then?

That prayer is really, really hard? And that we're not motivated to pray by beating ourselves up into a prayer-debt? And that guilt-tripping actually makes me want to pray less?

Maybe prayer is more than firing off theologically correct descriptions. Maybe it's a conversation with a person, one who really listens and answers.

Maybe it's a long-distance phone call to the one who loves our very soul, regardless of how far we've gone.

It's a reminder of our engagement to God before we meet Him face to face in that final Wedding of the Lamb; it's a raw moment of truth to discuss our daily uphill climb, with the one who made us, a time of healing from all the hurt we see and suffer every day.

Talking with Him, walking with Him.

When I think of prayer this way, I begin to miss Him. And when I pray to Him, even when I just messed up, those very moments become my most treasured memories. Hanging out with God, basking in His goodness, soaking in His glory, bowing at His robe, as close as a brother and grand like no other, a perfect union of reverence and intimacy.

He is holy, but so near.

I still remember the first time I really prayed without all the coercion. I had a six month season of migraines so bad that I would go nearly blind; I needed friends to help me walk because it felt like my eyeball was on fire. Medicine didn't help. I went in for a CT scan and there was nothing abnormal.

So I was on the ground one night with this migraine pressing against my optic nerves like a pick-axe grinding away, and I prayed. I couldn't see. I was trying not to cry but the tears came anyway. My head weighed a thousand pounds, my eyelids were curled up, and I was sweating through clenched teeth.

Pain has a way of making you embarrassingly honest. I was confessing sins I've never sinned. I was begging God for relief. I was making weird promises. I went on and on until I had nothing to say.

There was no grand eloquent speech. I didn't use formal language, like we so often hear the pastor doing. I was babbling, really.

It was right then, it felt like I was being steadied with calmness. I don't mean to sound too mystical and this isn't something I've tried to duplicate. I just knew He was there. He didn't acknowledge all my sputtering. It was simply His arms around me, holding me while I was on my knees, rocking back and forth, a Father who came down to the ground and embraced me in that moment of pain. He seemed to whisper, *I am here. I am here. My son, I am here.*

The pain didn't go away, but God and I—we had a great time.

I love Him for that. It took that sort of pain to really understand. But after the migraines ended, I kept talking to Him. I realized He was always there, rain or sun or in-between. Not "waiting" for me to talk, like the sermon chides, but just *there*. And He loves even our stumbling attempts at prayer, because He loves the mess inside. He can't help Himself.

Isn't this what we long for? A constant presence to fully know our craziness and still engage. That we are fully known and yet fully loved. Because we have that in Him. We have a God who became a man, who pro-foundly knows our pain, and wants not only to hear from us, but *talk* with us. To walk hand in hand and embrace us in every condition.

Maybe it's blasphemous, I don't know. I just know that I've found the desire to pray to Him when I quit worrying about technique and method and routine, and simply just want to know Him for who He is. He gives us the freedom to talk with Him in our messy, sloppy, flailing weirdness—and He probably prefers it.

We can be completely ourselves with Him, however imperfectly.

So I run to Him through distractions. I quit the guilt trips. I know that He works through prayer, even if I don't know how.

I can speak with words big or small, or none. At times He speaks; sometimes He doesn't; and both are okay. I love Him in good times, bad, through pain, through dryness—and He loves me through it too. He's singing that song over us right now. And indeed, I pray that us tiny earthly people can bring Him glory, and that He would rain down mercy and that His holy fire would fill us.

I pray because I love Him.

It's not that I can't do this alone without God.
It's that I wouldn't even want to.

God is at once
bigger than our minds can comprehend
and is closer than our hearts dare to believe.
He is huge, over all;
He is here, right now.

An Entire Life in 4 Minutes, 54 Seconds

I was at a funeral for an older gentleman and we were shown a video of his life from birth to death. We watched as he grew up from Kindergarten to high school to graduation to becoming a barber and an Air Force pilot and a husband and a father and then his battle with multiple sclerosis, which took his life with a stroke.

It was amazing to see him as a handsome, agile young man with a head of dark flowing hair and the posture of a superhero. Most of us didn't even know he was a barber. It was amazing to see the wedding photos, this couple growing old together, smiling all the way, his wife by his side to the very end.

The video was four minutes and fifty-four seconds long. An entire life, told through pictures, in less than five minutes.

As selfish as it seems, I wondered about my own video one day. I wondered how it would be sitting in a building watching my entire life in a slideshow.

I thought about what they would say about me, if some would say "He wasn't all he was hyped up to be" or "We lost an amazing person today" or "We disagreed often, and I loved him for it." I wondered if they would show that picture from third grade when I was at Disney

World wearing a giant Mickey Mouse hat with my brother pretending to eat him. Or that one the day after I got out of the hospital after swallowing a bottle of pills and losing thirteen pounds in three days over a girl. Or the one of me battling to the very last breath over some sickness, all youth behind me, my story at a close.

The pastor said every life cannot control the start or end of their book. But we write the in-between. It's between us and God and all the merging stories we find of love, heartache, heaven, laughter, doubts, and goodbyes. And the many, many pictures.

It's quick, you know. There are only so many highlights in that reel. I don't want my head to be somewhere else when I'm here. I want to be here, now. We think we have a while, but really, it's a few minutes. A few snapshots, and then it's gone.

Here's to celebrating you, and for the memories.

Dancing with Shoelaces in Knots

"A chaplain? What do you even do?" someone asks.

Usually I answer with the checklist stuff, because it sounds purposeful.

"Death and bereavement. Viewings. Living wills. Next-of-kin search. Find a surrogate. Bless babies. End-of-life support. Comfort families in the waiting room. Respond to a Code Blue. Pray."

And then I say, "Mostly, I talk with sick people."

To be truthful, the to-do list stuff is easier because it has tangible goals. It has an official air, with a definitive landing. But the talking part is weird and sloppy. It's like slow dancing with a stranger.

Dialogue has no rules about it, which sounds romantic, but imagine two people trying to dance for the first time with their shoelaces jammed up in knots, and the patient expects me to a be a professional when half the time I'm learning on the fly as I adjust to the patient's feet. It sounds cute but it's clumsy.

Imaging trying to start a conversation when:

Case 1 — A young man drives off a bridge. The paramedics find a gunshot wound in his side. It's possible he had been running from a drug bust gone bad. His entire family is notified; the man dies; the family is screaming at the top of their lungs in the waiting room.

Case 2 — A woman's husband has just died. She's handling it well. She even makes a few jokes next to her husband's body; she's had time to process his dying. But she's more upset that her husband's family is trying to grab at his will, his wealth, his house. The woman asks me what I can do.

Case 3 — An ex-convict has a body cast from head to toe. He believes that God might be punishing him. He confesses that he's killed a few people; he wants to kill someone when he's out of the hospital, but his sickness is changing his mind.

Case 4 — A boy under ten years old has been struck by a car. The boy is injured but recovering. His parents are taking shifts at his bedside; I walk in the room to find his mom. She's relieved it wasn't worse, but she's scared.

Case 5 — An elderly woman is dying. She has no home, her family is out of state, and she thinks she'll die alone. She asks me how to do a funeral, how to get right with God, how to reconcile with her husband.

Case 6 — A dying elderly man asks if it's morally right to prolong his own life on an artificial machine.

Case 7 — A woman has had five heart attacks, but she's not slowing down. Her two daughter are in the room, one who works at a hospital, and they're both concerned for their mother's health. She promises she wants to take care of herself, but her daughters are doubtful. They look to me for answers.

Do I tip-toe around their concerns? Or do I offer my opinion? Do I leave it open-ended? Or do I help them work it through?

I ask those questions all the time. I don't bring a scalpel or a syringe to the room. I only have words; I only bring myself.

And it's tough. Sometimes I step on toes. I say too much. I move too slow or too quick. I feel like I shouldn't have been there and I'm making it worse.

At times, when I really pay attention, I know that a miracle is growing. I cherish those moments, when we meet eyes, find that conversational tempo like a heartbeat, and we build something, pieces fitting into a finely layered edifice. You know what I mean: that sudden smooth stream when you and a friend have hit a pocket of chemistry where the talk flows freely, where each word becomes a warm rush of water over cold, weary hands. There's a graceful motion in lock-step, gliding a little closer to closure, and we untie some of those knots in our shoes, with no expectation but enjoying that tiny slice of time.

And it's not always the talking, but *being*. The stillness of listening. A face of sincerity. A laugh at the right time. A nod that says, *I hear you, and I'm here.*

After stepping on so many toes, I've learned there are two things the patients have in common. Two simple denominators that might be woven in all of us.

1) Everyone's hoping to go home.

2) *I'm* the constant in these rooms.

The dance comes together when I help each patient feel like they're home. Not home in the hospital, but home in their heads, their hearts, their hurts, right now. Everyone needs a familiar rhythm, a friendly face, the landmark that says *I'm in a place that I know.* That's the constant in every form of intimacy, really. We're looking for home in each other, an open door to the dance floor inside. This can be found even in a hospital gown, if someone's there to dance.

This Was It, My Closing Number

This patient had an accident at work and told me, "I thought this was it, chaplain, you know, my last moments there on the floor. I could feel it, life draining out like a long thread in circles, red just spreading wider. The guys got close to me, they put down their tools in a big clatter and took off their gloves and helmets and just gathered. I had worked with them for years and years, Brad and Tommy and Wes and Ryan, their kids came to my cook-outs, I got gifts for their birthdays. We built things together. There's no bond like that, nothing on earth ever better. I mean, these guys were my family— but I never talked to them about the God-stuff, my *faith*, the important stuff, you know? They thought maybe I was a little religious or something, like church was another part of the rigmarole, and I was embarrassed to be the church guy. I guess that don't matter when you're on the floor bleeding out like that. So I just started singing at the top of my lungs. *'All to thee, my blessed savior, I surrender all ...'* and I just sang and sang and my eyes closed but my lips kept moving. I thought this was it and I couldn't ... I wanted them to know Him, you know? It was all I cared about right then. I love those guys. They had to know. If I was going out, they had to know where I was going. And maybe, you know, they could get there with me."

"And we urge you, brothers,
warn those who are idle,
encourage the timid,
help the weak,
be patient with everyone."
— 1 Thessalonians 5:14

"Do nothing out of selfish ambition or vain conceit,
but in humility consider others better than yourselves.
Each of you should look not only to your own interests,
but also to the interests of others."
— Philippians 2:3-4

Tracing the Sunbeam
to the Son

On days like today, when I doubt God and doubt myself, I have to remember there were many days like this before and I got through them. He was there.

A lot of times I imagine God trying to get our attention with a startling beam of sunlight through a slit of glass in a dusty room while we're rushing on to the next thing, because He wants us to slow down and savor the life we won't ever get again. I think probably I've walked by that sunbeam too many times, drowning in the motion of my autopilot and darting past the perfect swirl of His canvas. But so He has enough grace to draw the twisting fleck of dust in the beam again.

Maybe one day soon we will know the artist of that persistent sun. In the silence we might find Him, in the darkness to embrace His certain grip in our trembling hand. In His grace we might crawl up that soft beam, where there is glory.

Pursuing God is about realizing more and more that He has been pursuing you all along, and slowly waking to this reality. It's knowing that every ounce of effort you've made towards Him has been His wooing grace, beckoning you ever closer.

Jesus and Mashed Potatoes

It was another night at the homeless ministry, but for some reason, this night, I was ridiculously giddy. I had two giant serving spoons and I slammed down big gobs of mashed potatoes and casserole to the two-hundred people in line. Each of them had their empty plates extended, with big smiles to match mine, and I nearly cracked their styrofoam plates in half. I just couldn't get over how happy I was to serve these wonderful people.

In the middle of scooping green beans and lasagna, as I laid down food on every eager plate, as I greeted each person with a giant goofy grin, I suddenly thought:

God—is this how You feel about us?

Are You this happy when you serve us?

Are You this pleased when we offer our empty plates to You?

Maybe that sounds cheesy, but I was so struck by the thought that I stopped for a few moments, looking at these arms stretched wide to receive provision. I loved them so much that my chest was about to cave in, and I thought how God must feel all the time, and I went to my car and wept. I thought about that song that God is singing over us, to the brim with barely containable joy, rejoicing as we call to Him, serving us His best, His Son, His breath, His life, and how He celebrates when we receive what He so graciously longs to give.

When you see what Jesus did
and believe who Jesus was,
you become like Jesus is
and do what Jesus does.

He Will Never, Ever Stop

Grace is not so much any one action or rule or attitude, but is more of a story about broken people being loved and healed: and this grace always comes at a price.

Let me tell you about my first pastor. When I first came to church over fifteen years ago, I was a stubborn, thick-headed atheist looking for "hot religious girls." I hated the sermons but I kept coming back, because there was something about this pastor.

He endured with me. I asked him tons of annoying questions about God and the Bible, but he answered them patiently. I screwed up, a lot. I confessed the worst of my sexual struggles, but he never flinched. He called me and texted me when I never replied. He bought me lunches, dinners, books, and sent cards to my house. He spent hours praying for me. He never once lost his temper with me.

Over time, I realized how much of a jerk I was to him. I didn't listen, I was late all the time; I got drunk and went to strip clubs on Saturday nights before strolling in hung-over on Sundays; I hardly asked how he was doing. But he was endlessly loving. And his patience completely melted me. Of course, there were times when he rebuked me, when he laid down the hard truth—but it was always with a shaking voice, with a gentle hand. There's no way I could be the person I am today without him.

I remember small moments. When one day I was horribly depressed, and he wrote me a letter right in front of me. When I got out of the hospital from swallowing a bottle of pills, and he listened without judging. When I was sobbing hysterically one day and he gripped both my hands and told me, *It'll be okay. God still loves you, and He will never stop.*

Even now, my eyes glisten and my heart swells at his sacrifice. *His grace fundamentally ripped away my selfishness and disturbed my ego.* I deserved nothing and he gave me his all.

But why was my pastor this way? Because of Jesus. The heart of my pastor was fueled by the heart of Christ. It all pointed to him, and as much as my pastor loved me, Jesus loves us infinitely more. *For all the ways my pastor endured with me, he was showing me a small glimpse of the outpouring love of the crucifixion, and the more I looked back on his reckless grace for me, the more that it punctured my heart and tenderized me.*

I began to understand that grace is a love-relationship, a journey, an adventure, a story of a restless human heart who can only find wholeness in Christ, who died the death of love that we might have such rest.

I trusted my guilt, my shame,
my self-pity to move me.
I grit my fists, clenched my teeth,
I reached for the person I should be.
Yet I could not be shamed into change,
because it only re-arranged my behavior.
I could not fundamentally break my ego,
for I was only restraining my nature.
I needed a new heart, a Savior.
Grace caught me:
by faith, He had already raised me,
and had moved me far much more
than I dared to believe.
For I forgot the price of grace to bring me back,
that cost His hands and feet.
I dared for a love stronger than all my shouting,
my sickness, my shadow in the mirror.
A love busting at the seams of my heart,
a new heart—
—a love that loosened my fists and my failure.

When I behold the glory of God: my problems are just problems and not the end of me. Nothing is the final sentence on us but His glorious grace.

When I behold the glory of God: people are just people and not receptacles to squeeze validation, nor standards to please. I can simply cherish them.

When I behold the glory of God: I can accurately estimate the little length of time I've been given on earth, and move by His pulse. No wait is too long, no work is unsung.

It's not that you were merely forgiven of sin by Christ.

It's that you're called to be so much more: for a mission specifically wired for you to heal your corner of the universe, to live a fully forgiven life that passionately seeks restoration in all the broken places. God saved you from sin, but He also made you for Him. He brought you from death to a real life, to not merely soak in but also pour out.

Will He forgive you no matter what?

Yes. And He hopes that such forgiveness will not merely bring you to the edge of the pit, but to climb with both feet into unexplored lands of adventure.

It isn't just about running away from the lesser things, but running towards the Greatest. At His feet, the volume of sin will decrease. He's that good.

The Jesus That I Need

The Jesus that I want would probably serve me and my own interests and align with my theological leanings and plans and dreams.

The Jesus that I need would serve the people that I forgot existed, who lived outside my best-laid plans and doctrinal camps, and he would just as quickly subvert my interests to care about others' interests above my own.

The Jesus that I want would probably listen to my music, look like my race, match my Myers-Briggs, and fight for my ideology.

The Jesus that I need would knock me over with exuberant music I never heard, enter my culture without condescending or conforming, would accept and challenge who I am, and transcend the very petty human idea of an ideology.

The Jesus that I want would probably die for people who liked me or were like me or were most likely.

The Jesus that I need died for the people who were nothing like him and he loved them, and even liked them, and he rose to find them. He even rose to find you and me: the least likely, because he's the love we want, and need.

Peter, Simon, Rock

Peter is not Peter's original name. His original name was Simon. Jesus had given him a nickname, "Peter," which in the Greek means rock. Jesus was telling him, "This is who I've called you to be. I want you to be strong, to be confident, to be who I've made you to be and saved you to be."

From looking at the four gospel accounts, whenever Jesus called Peter "Simon," Jesus was telling him that he was acting like his old self. I can imagine after a while, Peter would cringe when he heard "Simon." But whenever he got it right, Jesus called him "Peter."

I imagine Peter embraced his new name, and I believe God shapes each of us the same way. Jesus says that we were made for more, that we were created to do amazing things, that we are treasured, prized, and loved. When we go back to our old self, Jesus is saying, *"Come on, you're no longer Simon. You're now Peter. You're the Rock."*

Jesus knew everything Zacchaeus had done and still loved him.
It didn't change Jesus; it changed Zacchaeus.

Matthew Levi, Shadow Made Full

In the days of Jesus, young Israelite students went under the shadow of a rabbi and memorized the Old Testament by ten years old, and by fifteen, they could ask their rabbi, "Can I become your disciple?" The rabbi could either say, "You're not good enough, you don't have what it takes, go to your family business," or he could say, "Follow me."

In Mark 2:13-17, Matthew also had the family name Levi, which means he most likely descended from the Levitical priests like Moses, Aaron, Ezekiel, Ezra, and Malachi. So Matthew's family was banking on him becoming a disciple of a rabbi, because this was their family business, their entire hope for a future.

But when we meet Matthew, he's a hated tax collector, a sell-out of his own people. Which means Matthew's rabbi had told him, "You're not good enough." And Matthew had no other way to make a living.

I can just imagine that long walk home when he was turned down, Matthew's father seeing his son from the doorstep and realizing he didn't make it, backing into the house, the silent steps through the door. I can imagine Matthew's heartache, his rejection, and like the Prodigal Son, grabbing his inheritance to buy a tax collector's booth.

Then Jesus walks by Matthew's table, and in a moment predetermined before rabbis and schools and qualifications and the foundation of time itself, Jesus says the words that Matthew Levi has been waiting to hear his whole life: **"Follow me."**

Matthew was probably thinking, "Why? Why would you want me? I'm a screw-up. You don't know what I've done. I'm not good enough, I don't have what it takes. Not even my father wants me."

But Jesus, without a single question, without qualifying him, without telling him to clean up first, was telling him: "Levi, it's your mess-ups that qualify you for this kingdom of mine. It's because of your mess-ups that I want you. In my eyes, you **are** good enough. You do have what it takes. It's not because of what you've done. It's because of what I'm doing. Come on. **Follow me.**"

We hate surrendering, yet we surrender ourselves to something every single day. Nearly everything else we give ourselves to will consume more than it gives back; it does not have our best interests in mind; it drains us.

Every other master says, "Serve me or die," but Jesus is the only master who says, "I will die to serve you."

Everything else in the world says, "Follow me," and it'll cost you your whole life.

Jesus says, "Follow me," and it does cost you your whole life, but he also gives you the only true life.

You are called to carry the cross, deny yourself, kill your flesh, lose your life, and leave behind the world: but you are never alone in this.

The one who calls you to follow him is the very one who empowers you to follow. Grace will cost you your pride, greed, anger, lust, sorrow, and selfishness—and in turn you get endless joy, eternal life, intimacy with our Creator, and wild freedom to love. It feels like sacrifice because we are used to our way, but we give up what we never needed anyway. It remains the Best Deal in the Universe.

Around the Corner: A Second Wind

You've been in meltdown before, when the world felt unusually cruel and your insides collapsed and there weren't enough tears to cry through your heaving, convulsing sobs. Like the wind was uppercut out of your soul.

It's not pretty. Not like the movies. It's not dramatic or cathartic or ironic or Oscar-worthy—it's ugly, snot all over, face puckered in fifty places, bowled over with all kinds of noises spewing from your guts.

I was reading John 20, and Mary Magdalene was there too.

Now Mary stood outside the tomb crying.

I read this and grew horribly sad, imagining her hunched over and hopeless. Her world was punched through. I knew how she felt.

The man they called Savior, who had rebuked seven demons out of Mary and had been bathed by her family's precious perfume, was now just a cold lifeless body in an airtight tomb. Along with his body were the dreams of a different future.

Mary was demon-possessed, so she wasn't allowed to shop, marry, have friends, go to the Temple, or travel freely. She was one of those fringe losers on the edge of everyone's radar. Maybe Jesus would've changed all that: but they killed him on a dirty wooden cross.

Only—around the corner—something was happening.

The dream was not dead.

Mary turns to see two angels. They ask why she's crying. She laments over her Lord, whose body she thinks has been stolen. She doesn't understand yet.

She turns again and there is a gardener. He asks why she's crying. She thinks he knows where the body went. She doesn't understand yet.

Some of us live in this space—*we don't know yet*. We are sitting outside a broken dream weeping into our hands and watching the sand fall through tired fingers. It's gone. We can't possibly know how it will get better. God understands this. It's partly why He sent His Son— to turn back the clock on every fallen grain of sand.

Jesus, in a miraculous meta-cosmic reversal, finished the sentence of humanity with his resurrection. Entropy died. Tragedies no longer defined the end. On the grandest scale, hope weaved itself into broken human hearts and we were revoked every reason to fear.

Then on the smaller scale, for Mary Magdalene, and for you and for me—we await the miracle around the corner.

We lost our dream in a garden once. But the gardener is here.

He is alive: and so now, are we.

It could be that nothing around you gets better. But He is there, extending life within the swirling mess of a hostile world.

It could be that people around you don't change. But He is there, growing you to change when others do not.

It could be that you get stuck at that obstacle once more. But He is there, having already removed every obstacle between you and Him at the cross, empowering you for so much better than you think.

In your crushed swollen chest where the hurt pulls in: Christ comes to fill the broken places like so much water in cracked earth, new breath stretching your lungs, so we may thrive and bloom and stand on our shaking feet again.

Turn. He is there.

"Because I live, you also will live."
— John 14:19

'

I demanded God to explain Himself, to explain our suffering, so He went one further and entered our pain—and in a tomb, He initiated healing, the reversal of all that had ever gone wrong. I demanded a diagram, but He gave us a song.

We Bleed, All the Way Up

The patient really believed her cancer was somehow "God's amazing plan for my life." She went on to say the things I always hear: "He won't give me more than I can handle. Thank God we caught it early. God is going to use this for my good."

I get why we say these things, because we're such creatures of story that we rush for coherence. But even when such theology is true, I want to tell her that it's okay to say this whole ordeal is terrible and that it really hurts and that we live in a disordered, chaotic, fractured, fallen world where the current of sin devours everything, that bad things happen to model citizens, that nothing is as it's meant to be, and the people who don't catch the cancer early aren't well enough to thank God for anything, and that not every pain is meant to be a spiritualized, connect-the-dots lesson as if God is some cruel teacher waiting for us to "get it."

Pain doesn't always have to be dressed up as a blessing in disguise. God hears our frustration about injustice and illness: for He is just as mad at suffering as we are. He doesn't rush our grief. He bled with us, too, in absolute solidarity, and broke what breaks us in a tomb. He is the friend who meets us in our pain, yet strong enough to lead us through. I can only hope, in some small measure, to do the same.

I was there at the bottom
when everyone else left,
and He was the only one there.
When they say rock bottom,
you find He's the stone under your feet,
the dry ground in shaky seas,
the grace that does not leave.
When my mind wanders,
my heart remembers the rock.

The Last Page First

When I go to the bookstore, I'll grab books and read the last few pages. I want to know how it ends. I want to know where we end up. Hollywood executives always read the first and last page of a screenplay, and if the characters don't change, they toss the script. We inherently want a landing, a safe conclusion, a final punctuation on the sentence of life.

When I first read the Bible for myself, I started at Revelation. I wanted to know if everything was going to be okay. I heard about the Fall of Man and all the ugly things that happened in Genesis; I knew about the flood and the tower of Babel and the incest and the wars. In Revelation, I was overwhelmed. Everything was getting put right again. Justice was unrolling from Heaven, angels speaking with mere men, evil squashed to pieces, healing was all over the place. Since then, I read the Bible very differently. I know that the first page doesn't get to say everything about us, and we get a landing, a final sentence of victory. We get to win, because God does.

When I ask if God is good
I see a cross, an empty tomb.
What He writ large in the stars
is writ small for our wounds.
From the sky to my sin
He is re-making us again.
When nothing else is good,
He is the only one who is.

I wonder how they could yell
Barabbas instead of Jesus.
I wonder how they sang Hosanna
and days later, Crucify him.
I wonder how Pontius
could wash his hands of it,
as though a dirty conscience
could be so easily cleaned.

But—I am Barabbas, sinner set free.
I yell "Crucify him" as I sing praises with ease.
I am Pontius, who turned a blind eye to glory.
And yet, so Christ still died for me.
Still he died, where I should be,
a perfect love on that tree.

Nail-Pierced Hands Through Fortress Lungs

I think about my life before Christ, how I used to live for myself and I would do good to look good and get good back.

I think about how something was always missing then, like I would find a particular interest and it would almost click but the edges wouldn't catch and they'd just slide off the inside of my heart.

I think of how I objectified humans as blunt weapons for my secret dirty desires and planned out my next crime scene like an elaborate diorama: and all this to avoid the God who would speak to me at 3 am in the darkness when I couldn't lie to myself about the futility of my deceit. I remember how the ceiling fan would accuse me of guilt with its every cut into the sides of my lying mouth.

I think of those moments when the veil of shallow shadow-living was lifted for a blinding second, and my reality was torn open to the idea of a Creator and how there must be more than just collecting toys to build an empire until I die. It was only a glimpse, but everything else around it would be sterile and insignificant in comparison.

I remember the drawstrings of my cold protective fortress being tugged by gentle hands that plunged through my lungs, never too sharp, but just enough to know there was something else about this life that life was not telling me, that a cosmic problem existed with a solution that would click as easily as a key in butter.

I think of how even though I ran from Him—God still literally loved me to death and afflicted my selfish emptiness with a love that cost the blood of His only son.

I asked myself then, "Is it possible to miss someone you never knew about?" Because before I knew Him, I knew Him, and I dearly missed Him, if only in dreams and whispers and longings I could hardly stand to utter. I was terrified to discover that life wasn't about me. I was scared to find my Maker—but He found me, and now I cannot go back. I don't ever want to. I cannot imagine any other way without Him, and He does not imagine His story without me.

In darkness,
He rolls the stone away.
At your darkest,
He loves you anyway.

Suddenly Wanting His Return

Was driving today in a panic to take care of a million things, looking up at the spotty sky that looked like God had painted with a clogged spray-paint can. Tired, frustrated, irritated, jealous of everyone else who wasn't me.

Suddenly imagined Jesus with his one-hundred million angels, separating the spray painted clouds and his trumpets blasting and the entire earth lit up by his lightning-and-thunder presence. If one angel has a twelve foot wing span, then that's 11 miles of wings per one mile of sky. Imagine the sound.

It was a rush. To think at any moment the show could be over, the whole lid ripped off history and the director yelling cut. Justice finally unrolling itself in completion. Jesus here, in full glory, no more charades—his head on fire, a sword sticking out his face, stars in his hand, riding a war horse.

Hurry, Lord. Can't wait for the day.

Until then: we fight.

God is in control,
but do something.
Not because God isn't powerful,
but because He is.

Heaven, Hell, Golden Utensils

There's an old story that describes Heaven and Hell.

In Hell, there are long ornate tables topped with giant plates of freshly cooked food, as much as you can eat, with giant golden forks and spoons. The people attempt to eat with those huge utensils but they can't ever get the food in their mouths.

In Heaven, there are the same tables, the same food, the same golden utensils. And the people are eating with celebration and joy: because they're feeding each other.

I think we see glimpses of this every day, right now, because Hell is isolation and Heaven is meant to be shared. And I think they're not too far apart, because God did make all things for good, but it's our decision to use them for good or for evil. It is the orientation of our heart towards God and His kindness that bring us closer together: for the closer we are to an infinitely loving God, the less selfish we become.

I hope we will choose to get in that fun messy festive life of feeding each other.

A Reminder, Dear Christian

You are loved.

You might have heard that a million times, but it's no less true.

You do have a Creator.

He is with you.

He is bigger than your situation and closer than your deepest hurt. He's not mad. He is cheering for you and rooting for you this very second. He's okay about all the things before. He sent His Son for that very reason.

You can put down the blade. You can throw away the pills. You can quit replaying those regrets in your head. You can quit the inner-loop of self-condemnation. You can forget your ex. You can walk away from the porn. You can resolve your conflicts right now. You can sign up to volunteer at that shelter. You can thank your parents for everything. You can hug the person next to you. You can tell the waiter, "Jesus loves you." You can go back to church. You don't have to sit in the back. You don't have to prove your worth to the people you've let down. You don't have to live up to everyone else's vision for your life. You're finally, finally free.

You are loved.

I am loved.

As much as I love you, dear friend, He loves you infinitely more.

Believe it.

Walk in it.

Walk with Him.

God is in the business of breathing life into hurting places.

This is what He does.

"At one time we too were foolish, disobedient, deceived and enslaved by all kinds of passions and pleasures. We lived in malice and envy, being hated and hating one another.

But when the kindness and love of God our Savior appeared, he saved us, not because of righteous things we had done, but because of his mercy.

He saved us through the washing of rebirth and renewal by the Holy Spirit, whom he poured out on us generously through Jesus Christ our Savior, so that, having been justified by his grace, we might become heirs having the hope of eternal life."

— Titus 3:3-7

In Heaven,
there will only be one person with scars.
You'll have none
because he will have taken yours.

Upside-Down Valley:
Where the Mountain Touches the Sky
and Heaven Breaks Open

I can't imagine how difficult it must be to have lepro-sy. It was even worse in the first century.

You can't shop for groceries. You can't go to school or to church or get a job. You're never allowed to marry or to have children. No one wants to be friends with you, much less come near you. If someone approaches you on the street or walks past your doorway, you have to yell out, "I'm unclean." You're most definitely a beggar or living off family wealth.

If you had leprosy: you are untouchable, from your skin to your heart.

One day, you hear about a prophet who talks about the *Kingdom of God.* His name is John. He eats grasshop-pers and wears camels and cows. He's baptizing people in the water, actually *purifying* them in the Jordan. He keeps talking about someone greater who is coming, another Prophet whose feet were too worthy to touch.

You're a leper. You have a lot of time. You make the entire day's trip into town to get to the Jordan. The whole way, you're yelling, "Unclean, unclean, unclean." You lose a finger. A toenail falls off. You arrive at the Jordan at night, the stars heavy and the clouds just whispers. You hear the murmurs of hundreds, no, *thousands* of people in line by the side of the river. The moon is fragmented upon the surface, a wrinkled blue globe that has lit the faces of the weary.

Almost the moment you get there, a man in torn clothes says, "Behold! The Lamb of God who has come to take away the sins of the world!"

At first you think he's talking about you, and your stomach turns inside-out. But you can *feel* someone just past your shoulder, the crowds parting for him. You're used to this; the crowds have parted for you, too. Crowds have hissed at you, booed you, blamed you for your disease, said that you were cursed, blamed your parents and your ancestors and your lack of faith. Just seeing the lines of people move back puts a dull echo in your chest. Your illness touches every part of your life.

You see the man, this supposed Lamb of God. He walks through the split sea of people and enters the water. The man in torn clothes, John, is shaking. He is near hysterical. John blurts out, "You must baptize me." The Lamb-Man says, "No, John. You must baptize me. To fulfill all righteousness." For a moment, they have their hands on each other's shoulders. Everyone is fidgeting, frozen, waiting for their turn.

John dunks the Lamb in the water.

Then it happens.

You look up, and the moon twists in half. The stars scatter in every direction. The darkness swirls in blue and purple. You feel the river and the air reversing outward. A wind pushes through the Jordan and the water peels away and the people raise their arms gasping.

You haven't smelled a thing in years, but you catch the faintest hint of salt. You close your eyes for a moment, remembering. You are back there, with your mother, near the water when your hands could still build sandcastles. You are there, before your body began to waste away, piece by terrible piece, before this sickness stole you. You are there, your father raising you to the sun, above mountains and towards heaven, flying up and up to worlds unknown, when anything was possible.

Those dreams are just dreams. Gone, dust. But you remember.

You hear a low roar, louder and louder. Then the sky expands, breaks open, dances in circles, and a soft pouring light washes over John and the Lamb. The light is pulsing, like the wings of a bird suspended in time.

You hear a voice.

"You are my Son. It's you I love. With you, I am well pleased."

You're certain this voice is for the man who's being baptized. But you suspect that it could be for you, too.

The sky closes. The stars return. The wind dials down and the river is still. The moon is whole in the water again.

You look for the Lamb-Man, but he's gone. There's a sudden swell of conversation, but the line resumes and John continues to baptize.

You leave. You need to find this Lamb. You slink back through the streets, through the dark, saying "Unclean" without thinking, looking for this man. You know his face. You saw every detail under that glowing beam of heaven.

Over a month passes. You've been looking for him every day. There are rumors he has taken pilgrimage to the desert, which could mean he has died. Some say he went to fight the devil; others say he went to atone for his sin. You know plenty of sinners, but none of them could break the sky in half.

Then you hear the Lamb-Man is in town. You hear that he's been *healing diseases*. They say that about a lot of prophets. Anyone could be a messiah these days: just say you healed someone who was already getting better, and you're suddenly the Voice of God. You're skeptical. He could be another charlatan, a hustler, a fake.

It's not hard to find him. Everyone else in town is scrambling after him. You hear others saying, "Yeshua is here. The King. The Messiah."

You press through the people, yelling, "Unclean, unclean." The townspeople move back. As you get closer to the man they call Yeshua, you notice a small circle of men and women around him, but they're not moving away. They don't make a face at you. One of them even steps toward you.

You fall to your knees in front of Yeshua with your head bowed. You'll probably lose a toe. But with these prophets, you have to make a big show of everything.

You say, "If you are willing, you can make me clean."

Then you're jolted. You look up. The man Yeshua has actually *touched your shoulder.*

You look into his face. He is just a man. He is near tears.

He says to you, "I am willing. Be clean."

Another jolt, but this time it goes through your body. You look first at your hands. Your *hands.* You have all your fingers. You pull back your sleeves and your skin, your *skin,* you can feel your skin again. You touch your face and it's whole, it's there, everything is there.

Yeshua brings you to your feet. He says, "Please do not tell this to anyone. Show yourself to the priest and offer the sacrifices that Moses commanded for your cleansing, as a testimony."

And he hugs you. He kisses you on both cheeks. Your knees nearly buckle.

You are healed.

Of course, you have to tell everyone. You run through town, yelling, "Clean, clean!" You run to your family, to the market, to the church, running and running. "I'm clean! Yeshua has healed me!"

Soon you discover that the townspeople are rushing after the Lamb of God, taking to the streets in droves, looking for him. Yeshua and his circle of followers cannot stay; the crowds have grown too thick. They head to the next town.

You head back into town, to be restored again to the people.

A few years later, you hear they've accused this man of blasphemy, of claiming to be God, of revolting against Rome. He is sentenced to death.

You make the journey to Jerusalem. You love running now. You run to the Prefect's courtyards, the public square for judicial hearings. You hear that Pontius Pilate, the current Prefect of Rome, has ordered Yeshua to be flogged. It's the very worst sort of punishment that leaves a man in tattered bloody shreds. Somehow, Yeshua has survived the torture.

In the courtyard, dozens of people are shouting for crucifixion.

You're confused. This is the man who has healed hundreds of people. He tore open the sky. He taught the ancient words of Scripture. Even if he had been revolting against Rome, a crucifixion was an unspoken curse among men; it would mean you are completely untouchable, both here and in the afterlife.

Two Roman guards drag out Yeshua from behind the pillars of the court. He looks even worse than you imagined. His skin is hanging in flaps. Blood is still gushing from his body, his head, his chest. Some of his teeth are gone.

You remember this. When your teeth began to fall out. When your skin would flake and tear away.

You want to speak out against his murder: but the crowd is overpowering. You might be accused of being an accomplice. So you stay silent.

Pontius Pilate, dressed in the most ornate silver armor and purple robes, hushes the people. He says, "I have here two criminals." A second man is dragged out from behind the pillars, a man in chains. Pilate continues, "This man is the rabble-rouser Barabbas. He has killed Roman citizens and several of the Jewish family. This other man is Yeshua the prophet. He has done no harm that I can see. As customary to the Passover, I shall release one man back to you as amnesty for his sin. You may choose the man."

The people, without pausing, yell, "Barabbas."

You can hardly believe it. Pilate flinches and the guards are uncertain. In slow steps, they whisk Yeshua away, behind the pillars, to his death.

Barabbas is free. Yeshua is condemned.

You suddenly remember something. About the day Yeshua healed you.

He had asked you to re-instate your citizenship with the priest, so that you may be part of the community again. He had asked you not to tell anyone about the healing, but you did. From that day forth, Yeshua could not return to the town, but stayed on the fringes in solitary places.

I was able to walk freely in the town, but Yeshua was not.

He and I had switched places.

You are jolted again.

I am Barabbas. I am the sinner set free. I am Pilate, who turned a blind eye to glory.

You want to stop this madness, but they have taken Yeshua outside the city with a cross on his back, all the way to Golgotha, the Edge of the Skull. It is the hill of the damned.

You follow. You are familiar with slinking to the edge of the walls.

He is there. He is raised. He shouts. He is crucified.

You are seeing yourself, a twisted, mangled body, untouchable and unclean.

I am Barabbas. I am Pilate. I am the leper, made clean.

Yeshua is buried. The day is gone, and then another. It is quiet; the town has hushed. The disciples have ran, and you have forgotten the name of the crucified man.

But Sunday morning, you hear a small stirring.

There is a rumor.

There is a rumor that he is alive.

There is a rumor that Yeshua has appeared to many, with scars in his hands and feet, with a scar in the side of his heart. He has appeared even to his disciples, the ones who abandoned him, to restore them to God once again.

It would mean this healing is more than my body.

It would mean I can be healed for eternity.

You wonder if you should see.

You wonder.

It is just a rumor.

But oh, if the rumor was true.

If only it could be true.

Made in the USA
Middletown, DE
03 December 2017